CONTENTS

HOW TO USE THIS BOOK

JUST THE FACTS, INVENTIONS & DISCOVERIES is an easy-to-use, quick way to look up facts about inventions, inventors and famous discoveries. Every page is packed with names, places, dates and key pieces of invention information. For fast access to *just the facts*, follow the tips on these pages.

BOX HEADINGS
Look for heading words linked to your research to guide you to the right fact box.

INTRODUCTION TO TOPIC

TWO QUICK WAYS TO FIND A FACT:

1 Look at the detailed **CONTENTS** list on page 3 to find your topic of interest.

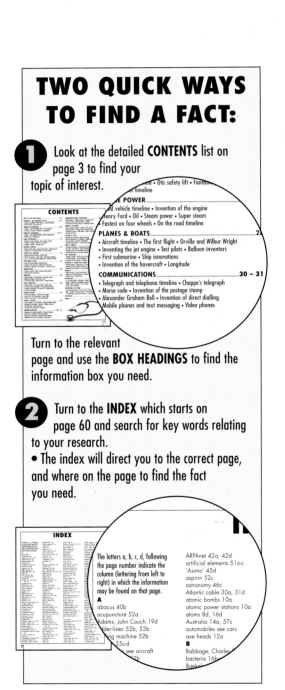

Turn to the relevant page and use the **BOX HEADINGS** to find the information box you need.

2 Turn to the **INDEX** which starts on page 60 and search for key words relating to your research.
• The index will direct you to the correct page, and where on the page to find the fact you need.

TELEGRAPH & TELEPHONE TIMELINE

1794 – Chappe's telegraph
Claude Chappe begins the construction of his telegraph across France.

1825 – Electro-magnet
The electro-magnet is invented. This is vital for the later invention of the telegraph.

1837 – Five-needle telegraph
William Fothergill Cooke and Charles Wheatstone invent the five-needle telegraph. It works by sending an electric current along wires which move two of the five needles, either left or right, so that they both point to one letter at a time.

1843 – Morse telegraph
Morse demonstrates his telegraph to the American Congress and they give him $30,000 to build a telegraph line from Washington D.C. to Baltimore, a distance of 40 miles.

The fax machine is invented by Alexander Bain.

1844 – Morse's message
Morse sends the first message on the new telegraph line. It reads, "What hath God wrought".

1858 – Atlantic cable
A cable is laid between America and Britain so that telegraphs can be sent across the Atlantic. The cable fails within a month.

1860 – First telephone
A German teacher called Philipp Reis invents a simple telephone. Reis builds just 12 telephones before he dies. One of Reis's telephones reaches Edinburgh University, and inspires a student called Alexander Graham Bell.

• *The TIMELINE continues on page 31.*

30

COMMUNICATIONS

When the American colonies declared their independence in 1776, it took 48 days for the news to cross the Atlantic. The arrival of the telegraph in 1843, and the telephone in 1876, meant that news could get to anywhere in the world almost instantly. The arrival of radio communication in 1896 meant that sounds could travel vast distances without the need for cables, and in 1936, moving pictures and sounds could be seen by millions, at the same time, with the invention of television.

Wheatstone and Cooke's five-needle telegraph.

CHAPPE'S TELEGRAPH

• In 1793, France was at war. A quick way to warn of an invasion was needed. In 1794, Claude Chappe invented the telegraph.

• Chappe's telegraph used two arms at the top of a tall tower. Ropes and pulleys moved the arms into different positions each representing a letter.

• The towers were positioned 10 to 30 kilometres apart and the messages were read by people using telescopes.

The main pole of the telegraph was about 6 metres tall.

MORSE CODE

• Samuel Morse invented Morse code in 1838. He first got the idea for the code in 1832 when he was told about experiments with electricity.

• Morse's idea was to develop a code based on interrupting the flow of electricity so that a message could be heard.

• Morse code works very simply. Electricity is either switched on or off. When it is on, it travels along a wire. At the other end of the wire the electric current can either make a sound or be printed out.

• A short electric current, a 'dit', is printed as a dot and a longer 'dah' is printed as a dash.

A –	N – •
B – • • •	O – – –
C – • – •	P • – – •
D – • •	Q – – • –
E •	R • – •
F • • – •	S • • •
G – – •	T –
H • • • •	U • • –
I • •	V • • • –
J • – – –	W • – –
K – • –	X – • • –
L • – • •	Y – • – –
M – –	Z – – • •

The full Morse code is based on combining dots and dashes to represent the letters of the alphabet.

• See page 48 SAMUEL MORSE.

THE INVENTION OF THE POSTAGE STAMP

• In the early 1800s, postage in Britain was charged by distance and the number of sheets in a letter. The recipient paid for the postage not the sender.

• In 1837, retired English schoolteacher Rowland Hill wrote a pamphlet calling for cheap, standard postage rates, not charged by distance.

• The British Post Office took up Hill's ideas, and, in May 1840, issued the first adhesive, penny, postage stamps.

• The stamps were printed with black ink and become known as 'Penny Blacks'.

PICTURE CAPTIONS
Captions explain what is in the pictures.

JUST THE FACTS
Each topic box presents the facts you need in short, quick-to-read bullet points.

4

JUST FACTS

INVENTIONS & DISCOVERIES

By

Dee Phillips

Brian Alchorn, Catherine Chambers, David Dalton,

Dougal Dixon, Ian Graham, Colin Hynson,

Clint Twist and Richard Walker

ticktock

First published in Great Britain in 2006p by **ticktock Media Ltd.**,
Unit 2, Orchard Business Centre, North Farm Road, Tunbridge Wells, Kent, TN2 3XF
ISBN 1 86007 860 5 pbk
Printed in China
A CIP catalogue record for this book is available from the British Library.

We would like to thank: Wendy and David Clemson, Evelyn Alchorn, Steve Owen and Elizabeth Wiggans.

Picture credits t=top, b=bottom, c=centre, l-left, r=right
Adidas: 35tr. Alamy: 13cb. Ancient Art and Architecture: 13ct. Corbis: 8tr, 9br, 16b, 17t, 22b, 24b, 27tl, 27bl, 27cb, 29t, 29bc, 32b, 33c, 39tc, 41tl, 41cl, 50t, 51t. Dayton and Montgomery County Public Library, Ohio: 8cb. George Eastman House: 49b. Fujitsu Limited: 44b. Heritage images: 6c. Image Select: 26tr, 26br, 27tc, 28bc, 31t, 31tc. Louvre Museum, Paris: 12. Roslin Institute: 17b. Sandia National Laboratories: 45. Science Museum, London: 41lb. Science & Society Picture Library: 26c, 48c. Science photo library: 7br, 19b, 50cb, 51b, 53br. Sony: 44c. Springfield Library, Massachusetts: 7cb.

Every effort has been made to trace the copyright holders, and we apologise in advance for any unintentional omissions. We would be pleased to insert the appropriate acknowledgements in any subsequent edition of this publication.

2

6-11 Inventions Timeline

46-51 Inventor Biographies

BIOGRAPHIES

Throughout this book you will find biographies of famous inventors and scientists detailing all the key facts about their lives and work.

You will also find a chapter of biographies beginning on page 46.

ALEXANDER GRAHAM BELL 1847 – 1922

Nationality: Scottish-born American
Profession: Teacher and inventor

Biographical information:
Bell left school at 14 and trained in the family business of teaching elocution. His family moved to Canada in 1870. He trained people in his father's system of teaching deaf people to speak.

Most famous invention: Working at night with his assistant, Thomas Watson, he made the first working telephone in 1876.

Inventors at work: The telegraph already used electricity to convey messages over long distances. The telephone had to turn sound into electricity and back again. To make it work was a technical challenge, which Bell and Watson solved by hard work over many months.

Eureka moment: The first words spoken down a telephone were, "Mr Watson, come here, I want you!" Bell was testing out his newly invented telephone when he spilt some chemicals on his clothes and called to his assistant for help.

Alexander Graham Bell opens the New York to Chicago telephone line in 1892.

Bell experimented for many years with different ways of sending and receiving spoken messages. This *Gallows Frame* transmitter was one of his earliest machines.

THE INVENTION OF DIRECT DIALLING

- At first, telephone connections were made by operators pushing plugs into sockets.

- In 1889, in Kansas City, USA, undertaker Almon Strowger discovered that his local operator was married to a rival undertaker and was diverting his customers' calls to her husband.

- Strowger invented the first automatic telephone switch – a remote controlled switch that could connect one phone to any of several others by electrical pulses without the need for an operator!

MOBILE PHONES AND TEXT MESSAGING

1973 – First mobile call
The first call made on a mobile phone was made in April by Dr. Martin Cooper, general manager of Motorola. He called his rival, Joel Engel, Bell Laboratories head of research.

1992 – First text
The first text message was sent. It is reported that the message was from Neil Papworth of Vodaphone and it said, "Merry Christmas".

2000 – Camera phone
The camera phone is created by SHARP in Japan. It is called the J-Sh04.

August 2001
The first month in which over one billion text messages were sent by mobile phones.

VIDEO PHONES

- The first videotelephone with a screen for moving pictures was invented by AT&T in 1964. It allowed people to look at the people they were calling.

- Using mobile phones to record videos started with the creation of 3G mobile phones by Dr Irwin Jacobs in 2003.

TELEGRAPH & TELEPHONE TIMELINE

1861 – The pantelegraph
The first fax machine is sold. It is called the pantelegraph.

Telegraphs can be sent from one end of America to the other.

1865 – Public fax
The first fax service opens in France. It is used to send photographs to newspapers.

1866 – Atlantic cable
The ship, the 'Great Eastern', lays a second cable along the Atlantic seafloor.

1876 – Bell's telephone
Alexander Graham Bell invents the first successful telephone.

1878 – Thomas Edison
American inventor Thomas Edison has also been working on a telephone, but Bell beats him to it! Edison invents a microphone that makes the voice of the person speaking much clearer to the listener.

1880 – First pay phone
The first pay-phones open in New York.

There are now nine separate cables between America and Britain.

1892 – Direct-dial
The first direct-dial telephones become operational.

1915 – First Atlantic calls
Telephone calls across the Atlantic can be made for the first time.

1936 – Co-axial cable
The first co-axial cable is laid. This allows lots of telephone messages to pass along the same cable.

1963 – 160 Million phones
The number of telephones in the world reaches 160 million.

1988 – Fibre-optic cable
The first fibre-optic cable is laid across the Atlantic. Now telephone messages are carried on pulses of light.

• For more information on Edison:
• See page 36 EDISON'S PHONOGRAPH.
• See page 49 THOMAS ALVA EDISON.

31

TIMELINES

Important events are listed in chronological order.

For fast access to facts in the timelines, look for key words in the headings.

1876 – Bell's telephone...

LINKS

Look for the purple links throughout the book. Each link gives details of other pages where related or additional facts can be found.

• For more information on Edison:
• See page 36 EDISON'S PHONOGRAPH.
• See page 49 THOMAS ALVA EDISON.

GLOSSARY

• A GLOSSARY of words and terms used in this book begins on page 58.
The glossary words provide additional information to supplement the facts on the main pages.

AN AMAZING STORY...

Ever since Stone Age people invented simple tools for digging and cutting, inventions have changed the way humans live. Throughout history our natural curiosity about the world around us has led us to search for more information about our planet and our ancestors. The timeline on these pages tracks the last 250,000 years and looks at some of the groundbreaking moments in human history.

What secrets are still to be discovered about our planet and our ancestors?

250,000 BC

STONE TOOLS
Paleolithic (Early Stone Age) humans make simple stone tools, such as hand axes, by flaking a piece of flint from a large stone then chipping away smaller flakes to create sharp edges for cutting.

A flint hand axe, c 250,000 BC.

C 30,000 BC

BOWS AND ARROWS
Cave paintings from 30,000 BC onwards show 'Late Stone Age' humans using bows and arrows to hunt animals. Hunters also use a variety of snares and traps.

THE FIRST CLOCKS

Long before there were clocks, people relied on regular, natural events to keep track of time. They worked, ate and slept according to the rising of the sun. Over time, people invented many ways to track the passing of time.

WATER CLOCKS c AD100
Water ran through this ancient Chinese clepsydra, or water clock, over a set period of time. As each section of the staircase-like timepiece emptied, people knew an exact amount of time had passed.

A clepsydra or water clock

CANDLE CLOCKS c AD 800
When candles were used for telling the time, they were often divided up into sections that each took an hour to burn.

SUNDIALS
For hundreds of years, people have used sundials to tell the time. The sundial's gnomon (pointer) casts a shadow onto a scale marked on the flat base. The scale shows the hours of the day.

PENDULUM CLOCKS
In the 1650s, there was a great breakthrough in timekeeping when a Dutch scientist, Christiaan Huygens built the first pendulum clock.

Huygens designed a mechanism which used the swing of a pendulum to control the rotation of weight-driven gearwheels inside the clock. This use of the pendulum had originally been thought of by the mathematician Galileo Galilei.

• See page 47 GALILEO GALILEI for information on Galileo and pendulums.

C 3000 BC

WRITING
The Sumerians of southern Mesopotamia invent writing. Mesopotamian texts, still in existence today, range from simple lists of goods, to complex stories and the laws that governed the Sumerians' society.

Model of a Mesopotamian wheeled-vehicle, c 2000 BC.

AD 200

ROMAN CENTRAL HEATING
The Romans build villas and public baths using central heating systems called 'hypocausts'. Heat from fires is drawn into an open space under the floor; the heat then rises through the floor into the walls.

1400

CANNON
In Asia, bamboo-tube guns were produced which used gunpowder to shoot arrows. By 1400, metal cannons that fire stone cannonballs are in use across Europe.

1608

TELESCOPES
Hans Lippershey invents the telescope. Italian scientist, Galileo, builds his own telescope in 1609 and makes many new astronomical discoveries – the future for Lippershey's invention is secured!

Galileo's telescope

Tool making dates back even further than this timeline, to *Homo habilis (handy man)* who lived 2 million years ago.

9000-7000 BC ►

THE FIRST FARMERS
People discover that domesticating animals such as sheep and goats gives a more regular meat supply than hunting. Cultivation of crops such as wheat and barley begins.

C 7000 BC ►

MAKING FIRE
Neolithic people discover how to make fire. They make simple tools for producing friction and use flints struck against rocks called pyrites to cause sparks.

C 3500 BC ►

THE WHEEL
Wheels are first used in Mesopotamia (modern-day Iraq) as a turntable for making pottery. By 3500 BC, vehicles are in use that have solid wheels made by joining two or three wooden planks together in a disc shape.

C 2500 BC ►

GLASS
Glass is made by heating sand with limestone and wood ash. The method for making glass is probably discovered by accident. Ancient Egyptian glass beads have been found from around 2500 BC.

C 2000 BC ►

CHARIOTS
On the southwestern fringes of the Asian steppes the lightweight, two-wheel, two-horse chariot is developed. Chariots quickly become prestige war-vehicles used by civilisations such as the ancient Egyptians.

An ancient Egyptian wall carving which shows a chariot.

C 1000 BC ►

GREEK ALPHABET
The ancient Greeks use a 24–letter alphabet adapted from the Phoenician alphabet. Each symbol in an alphabet represents a sound rather than a word. This is quicker to learn and easier to use than earlier pictogram writing systems.

A cannon and cannonballs

► 1455 ►

First printing press
German craftsman Johannes Gutenberg develops movable type and designs and builds the first printing press. In 1455, Gutenberg prints his first book, a Latin bible.

A page from the Gutenberg Bible.

THE ATOMIC CLOCK

The atomic clock was invented by English physicist Louis Essen in the 1950s.

- Atomic clocks use the energy changes that take place in atoms to keep track of time.

- Atomic clocks are so accurate they lose or gain no more than a second once every two or three millions years!

The US NBS–4 atomic clock.

1756 ►

CHEMISTRY
The English Scientist Joseph Black discovers the gas carbon dioxide when he notes that a substance in exhaled air combines with quicklime in a chemical reaction that can be reversed by the application of heat.

1772-1774 ►

OXYGEN
Two scientists working independently discover oxygen – Swedish chemist Carl Wilhelm Scheele, in around 1772, and English chemist Joseph Priestley in 1774.

1770s-1780s

STRUCTURE OF WATER
French chemist Antoine-Laurent Lavoisier discovers that water is a chemical combination of two gases that are found in air, hydrogen and oxygen.

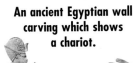

The idea of forming sheets of paper from macerated tree bark, hemp, rags and fishnets was conceived in China around 100 BC.

Without the invention of paper and printing it would not have been possible to produce this book!

c 1770 BC — Minoan printing
The Minoans invent the first known printing method. They use a writing system of 45 symbols, which are punched into a disk of clay before baking it. Only palace scribes could read and write, so Minoan printing was probably only used for tax lists and royal propaganda.

c 200 BC — Punctuation
Early Greek writers did not even use spaces between words. Aristophanes of Byzantium, the librarian at the Library of Alexandria is the first person to use punctuation in around 200 BC. He adds it to Greek text.

c 100 BC — Invention of paper
Cai Lun, (Ts'ai Lun), an official at the Chinese royal court is credited with the invention of paper.

c AD 350 — First books
Books with pages, known as codexes, become the standard way of storing words.

600 — Block printing
Paper is pressed onto blocks on which text has either been carved or hand written.

1403 — First metal font
Korean King Htai Tjong has the first true metal type-font made – 100,000 bronze characters are cast.

1455 — First movable type
German Johannes Gutenberg invents a technique for mass-producing individual metal letters. The text is assembled letter by letter to make up a page, an oil-based ink is applied and paper is then pressed against it to make a print. The type is then reassembled for the next page.

1464 — Roman type
German printers Adolf Rusch, in 1464, then Sweynheim and Pannartz in 1465, seeking to avoid the heavy, spiky letters of early types first use a *roman* font – the forerunner of the type this book is printed in.

• See page 48 JOHANNES GUTENBERG

1794

COTTON
In the USA, the engineer Eli Whitney patents his invention, the 'cotton gin', a machine that combs the seeds out of cotton after it has been harvested.

Slaves work at a Whitney cotton gin.

The *Locomotion* pulled 28 coal-filled wagons on the new Stockton and Darlington line.

1838-1839

CELLS
In 1838 to 1839, German scientists Matthias Schleiden and Theodor Schwann conclude that all plants and animals are made from tiny building blocks called cells.

1900

FINGERPRINTING
British scientist Francis Galton and police officer Sir Edward R. Henry devise a system of fingerprint classification which they publish in June 1900. The Galton-Henry system is used in the UK for criminal identification from 1901 onwards.

A fingerprint

Wilbur and Orville Wright

1908

THE MODEL T
The first Model T car is produced by the Ford Motor Company. Revolutionary production methods will see 15 million Model Ts role off the Ford assembly line over the next 19 years.

1927

EXPANDING UNIVERSE
While studying recently discovered galaxies outside of the Milky Way, Edwin Hubble discovers that the galaxies seem to be moving away from the Milky Way. This leads to the discovery that the universe is expanding.

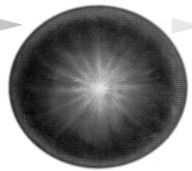

An expanding universe

1796 ▶

VACCINATION
British doctor Edward Jenner discovers the process of vaccination and successfully vaccinates a small boy against smallpox, a devastating disease in this period. The number of smallpox cases fall rapidly in the years following Jenner's discovery.

1822 ▶

MECHANICAL COMPUTER
Computer pioneer Charles Babbage, an inventor and professor of mathematics, conceives the first mechanical computer. However, the technology to build it will not be available for many years.

1824 ▶

BRAILLE
Frenchman Louis Braille invents an alphabet that can be written and read by the blind. The alphabet has 63 characters.

1825

FIRST RAILWAY
The Stockton and Darlington Railway, the first railway in the world to carry freight and passengers using steam traction, begins operation in England on 27 September.

An animal cell

1876 ▶

THE TELEPHONE
In March 1876, Scottish-born, American inventor Alexander Graham Bell is granted what is often said to be one of the most valuable patents ever – US Patent No. 174,465 for the development of a device to transmit speech sounds over electric wires.

1877 ▶

THE PHONOGRAPH
The first sound recording is made on a machine called a phonograph. American inventor Thomas Edison records himself reciting the nursery rhyme, 'Mary had a little lamb'.

1882

FIRST POWER STATION
American inventor Thomas Edison supervises the laying of mains and installation of the world's first power station in New York. It becomes operational in September 1882.

1901 ▶

MARCONI'S MESSAGE
Italian physicist, Guglielmo Marconi creates a worldwide sensation when he successfully sends a radio message across the Atlantic Ocean on 12 December. The message is dot dot dot, Morse code for the letter 'S'.

1903

FIRST FLIGHT
The Wright brothers achieve the world's first powered flight with their 'Flyer' biplane on 17 December. The flight covers 36.5 metres and lasts just 12 seconds.

1913 ▶

ATOMIC STRUCTURE
Danish physicist Niels Bohr proposes his theory of atomic structure – that an atom consists of a nucleus surrounded by a cloud of orbiting electrons arranged in a series of concentric outer shells.

1926

TELEVISION
British television pioneer, John Logie Baird, gives his first public demonstration of a television system. He presents moving pictures of a face. The pictures are fuzzy, but amazing at the time!

1941 ▶

PLUTONIUM (Pu)
The synthetic, radioactive element plutonium is made at Berkeley, California, by a team of scientists using a cyclotron. Plutonium is used as an ingredient in nuclear weapons and as a fuel in some types of nuclear reactors.

1943

COLOSSUS
During World War II, Alan Turing and a team of British scientists secretly build 'Colossus' (one of the first electronic computers) to decipher top secret messages created by the German 'Enigma' coding machine.

TIMELINE: INVENTION OF PHOTOGRAPHY

Thanks to the invention of photography, this book is packed with photographs of inventors and their inventions!

1826 - First photograph
In France, Joseph Niepce produces the world's first true photograph (as opposed to shadowgraph). The exposure time is about 8 hours.

1839 - Daguerreotype system
In France, Louis Daguerre demonstrates his daguerreotype system that produces a single positive image on a sheet of copper. Exposure time is 30 minutes.

1841 - Negatives
In England, William Talbot patents his calotype process that produces a negative image from which numerous positive copies can be made. Exposure time is 2 to 3 minutes.

1851 - Glass plates
1851 – in England, Frederick Archer introduces glass plates for photography. Exposure time is a few seconds.

1874 - Roll film
In the USA George Eastman develops roll film – first using paper, then later transparent celluloid. Exposure time is less than one second.

1888 - Kodak camera
Eastman launches the Kodak camera which produces circular images.

1941 - First colour film
In France, Auguste and Louis Lumière produce the first film for colour transparencies.

1942 - First colour prints
In Germany, the Agfa Company produces the first film for colour prints.

1946 - Instant prints
In the USA, Edwin Land introduces a camera that makes instant prints.

A Daguerreotype camera (1839)

• See page 49 GEORGE EASTMAN

Archaeologists can work out the age of this Egyptian mummy by using Willard F. Libby's discovery of the carbon dating process.

1946-1947 ▶

CARBON DATING

American chemist Willard F. Libby discovers that the unstable carbon isotope C14 decays over time to the more stable C12. This means plant matter or the body of an animal can be dated by the proportion of C14 compared to C12 left in it.

1947 ▶

THE TRANSISTOR

Three American physicists William B. Shockley, John Bardeen and Walter H. Brattain, invent the transistor – the device that will advance electronics, and allow for the miniaturisation of computer circuitry.

NUCLEAR POWER

FISSION

Fission is the process by which the nucleus of an atom is split in two releasing a large amount of energy. The fission of uranium atoms was first observed under laboratory conditions in the late 1930s.

CHAIN REACTION

On 2 December, 1942, a team of scientists led by Enrico Fermi achieved the first controlled nuclear fission chain reaction. Fermi realised their discovery could be used to build an atom bomb.

MANHATTAN PROJECT

During World War II, a team of scientists in the USA worked on the top-secret *Manhattan Project* to design and build atom bombs. The first bomb was tested at Alamogordo Air Base, New Mexico, on 16 July,1945. In the following month, two atom bombs were dropped on the Japanese cities of Hiroshima and Nagasaki.

NUCLEAR POWER

Uranium fission can be contained and controlled inside a nuclear reactor to produce heat for generating electricity. The first atomic power station making electricity for homes and businesses began operation in 1956 at Calder Hall in England.

• See page 51
ENRICO FERMI.

1969 ▶

SUPERSONIC AIRLINER

On 2 March, the Concorde, a passenger aircraft capable of flying at twice the speed of sound, makes its first test flight piloted by chief test pilot Andre Turcat. Concorde was a joint achievement between French and British engineers.

Concorde

1983 ▶

HIV VIRUS

The HIV virus that causes AIDS is identified by French scientist Luc Montagnier and a team working at the Pasteur Institute in Paris.

1984 ▶

DNA PROFILING

English scientist Alec Jeffreys invents a method of analysing DNA to produce a set of characteristic features that are unique to each individual. The process is called DNA profiling and can be used to identify criminals, or eliminate innocent crime suspects.

Alec Jeffreys, inventor of DNA profiling

1996 – Dolly the sheep is born.

2003 ▶

THE HUMAN GENOME

The Human Genome Project completes the task of reading in sequence all the 'letters' in the human genome (the set of instructions to build a body which are contained inside every body cell).

A hydrogen bomb (which is more powerful than an atom bomb) was first tested by the USA in 1951.

1952
DNA DISCOVERIES
American biochemists Alfred Hershey and Martha Chase demonstrate that DNA is the means by which genetic information is transmitted. In 1953, Crick and Watson discover the structure of DNA.

DNA

1967
FIRST HEART TRANSPLANT
On 3 December, a team of 20 surgeons led by South African heart surgeon Christiaan Barnard perform the world's first heart transplant at the Groote Schuur Hospital, Cape Town, South Africa. The patient Louis Washkansky lives for 18 days.

1974
LUCY
Professor Donald Johanson and his assistant Tom Gray discover the most complete Australopithecus skeleton ever found during excavations in northern Ethiopia. Nicknamed Lucy, this early hominid lived 3.2 million years ago.

1975
MICROSOFT
Bill Gates and his friend Paul Allen start Microsoft. The company creates the operating system MS-DOS and Windows. These programmes will be used on almost every PC in the world.

Bill Gates

1991
WORLD WIDE WEB
The World Wide Web is launched to the world via the Internet. It was invented in 1989 by British computer scientist Tim Berners-Lee for use at a scientific research facility.

www – World Wide Web

1996
DOLLY THE SHEEP
A team of scientists working in Scotland at the Roslin Institute succeed in producing the first ever cloned mammal. Dolly the sheep is born on 5 July.

2000
DRAFT HUMAN GENOME
A first draft of the human genome is published after more than 10 years of intensive effort. It consists of some three billion pairs of nucleotide bases divided into thousands of separate genes.

2004
A NEW PLANET
On 15 March, NASA announces the discovery of a new planet at the far boundaries of our solar system. The planet, named Sedna, has a diameter of 1600 km.

**Sedna takes over 10,000 years to orbit the sun.
Many scientists do not yet agree that Sedna is a planet.**

DEVELOPMENTS IN MATHEMATICS

Place Value
The use of '0' for zero probably dates from c 500 AD. This marks the emergence of the decimal system we use today.

Decimal fractions
Though used in China in around AD 200, decimal fractions were not developed in other parts of the world until the 1300s to 1400s.

Algebra
The word 'algebra' comes from a book by Al-Khwarizmi, an Arab mathematician who lived around AD 780-850. The most famous algebraic equation is Einstein's:

$$E=mc^2$$

Imperial measures
Standard Imperial Units of distance (for example the mile) were set by Queen Elizabeth I in 1592.

Metric measures
The metre, litre and gram were adopted by the French in 1795.

Pythagoras' theorem
Pythagoras lived c 580-500 BC. His theorem says that the square drawn using the longest side of a right angle triangle is equal in area to the sum of the areas of the triangles on the other two sides. This theorem can be used in navigation, maps, building and land measurement.

This diagram shows Pythagoras' theorem.

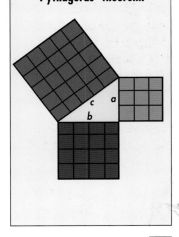

Burins, engraving tools made from a flint with a sharp edge, are used to decorate bone and wooden items.

Wooden handles are attached to stone tools for the first time making it possible to hit things harder, and to increase the amount of swing achieved with a tool such as an axe.

c 30,000 BC – Rope

Rope braided from plant fibres is used for making nets and snares for catching animals.

c 9000 BC – First ovens

The first known ovens, stone or clay chambers heated by a fire, are in use in Jericho in ancient Palestine.

c 8000 BC – Flint mining

When people can no longer find enough flints on the ground around them for tool-making, they begin to dig for stones under the surface – mining is invented.

c 7000 BC – Flax and linen

The flax plant is cultivated for its fibres which can be used to make ropes and linen.

c 6000 BC – Axe heads

Stones are shaped to create axe heads (as we would recognise them today) with a straight, sharp edge and a heavy base.

c 5500 BC – Weaving

The weaving of baskets develops: split bamboo is used in China, straw and flax in the Middle East and willow in Europe.

c 5000 BC – Leather

It is discovered that animal skins can be useful if they are dried and preserved using substances such as urine.

c 5000 BC – Grindstones

Grindstones (two stones which fit together) are used to crush cereal grains. This produces flour which is easier to digest than whole grains.

• See page 6 STONE TOOLS.
• The TIMELINE continues on page 13.

EARLY INVENTORS

O ver thousands of years our earliest ancestors invented and discovered ways to make their lives more comfortable and more interesting. They developed farming to ensure a regular supply of food, they devised tools and simple machines to make work more efficient, and they conceived ways of recording their lives, such as painting and writing, without which it would be impossible to chart the history of human invention and discovery.

EARLY FARMING INVENTIONS AND DISCOVERIES

5000 BC – The scratch plough
The wooden scratch plough (for breaking up the soil) comes into use. They are probably pulled by donkeys.

4000 BC – The sickle
Bone-handled sickles with a flint blade are used to reap wheat and barley.

3000 BC – The shaduf
The ancient Egyptians use a shaduf (a bucket on a weighted pole) to lift water from irrigation canals to water their crops.

2000 BC – Pollination
The discovery that there are male and female plants makes it easier to select crops for size, taste and disease-resistance by artificial pollination.

AD 500 – Three-piece ploughs
The development begins of heavy, iron, three-piece ploughs. They usually have wheels and are pulled by large farm horses. This type of plough enables farmers to work heavier soils and plough faster.

AD 500 – The horse collar
The development of the horse-collar enables a horse to pull a heavy plough without choking.

AD 800 – Three field system
In north-eastern France the three field system is developed. One field is planted in autumn with winter wheat or rye; the second field is planted the following spring with barley, peas or oats (to feed horses); the third field is left fallow (to rest).

• See page 7 THE FIRST FARMERS.

This ancient Egyptian wooden model dates to around 2000 BC. It shows a farmer using a simple scratch plough pulled by oxen.

DISCOVERING AND INVENTING METAL

Archaeologists have studied metal artefacts to work out when ancient civilisations first discovered metals such as bronze and iron.

COPPER 8000 – 6500 BC
The discovery of copper gave early humans a practical and more beautiful substitute for stone. Found naturally in its metallic state, copper's malleability made it easy to shape.

LEAD 6500 BC
Early metalworkers extracted lead by heating lead ore (stone containing lead) in a hot fire. Decorative lead beads, from around 6500 BC, found in Turkey suggest that lead was considered a precious material.

BRONZE 3500 BC
Ancient metalworkers melted copper and tin together and created a new

metal called bronze. This new material could be cast to make weapons and decorative items.

IRON 2000 BC
Iron was extracted from iron ore (stone containing iron) by heating the ore in red-hot charcoal. Iron is hard to melt, so early metalworkers developed new techniques such as hammering hot iron into the required shape.

THE INVENTION OF WRITING

THE FIRST WRITING

The Sumerians (who lived in what is now southern Iraq) had invented writing by around 3000 BC. They used a piece of reed to make cuneiform symbols (wedge-shaped marks) in clay tablets. Then they baked the tablets to harden them. The symbols were used to keep records of trade and taxes.

HIEROGLYPHS

The ancient Egyptians also discovered writing soon after 3000 BC. They used hundreds of pictures called hieroglyphs to represent words and sounds. They carved inscriptions on temple walls, painted on the walls of tombs, and wrote on papyrus paper.

CHINESE PICTOGRAMS

The ancient Chinese began writing around 1700 BC. They used a different pictogram (symbol) to represent each word — there were thousands to learn! Scribes used a brush to paint ink onto wood, silk and, in later times, paper.

中国

• See page 7
THE GREEK ALPHABET.

THE INVENTION OF PAINTING

Ancient paintings dating to around 30,000 BC have been found in caves in western Europe.

Prehistoric artists not only invented painting, they also invented paint made from minerals, such as chalk and red iron oxide; simple brushes made from chewed twigs or animal hair; and lamps which burned animal fat to light the dark interiors of the caves where they worked.

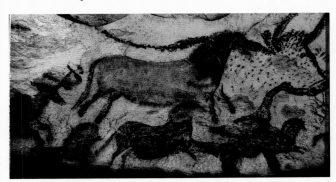

The artworks in the Lascaux caves in France (above) have been dated to around 15,000 BC.

LASCAUX CAVE PAINTINGS

Discovered:	12 September, 1940
Discovered by:	Marcel Ravidat, Jacques Marsal, Georges Agnel and Simon Coencas, four teenage boys exploring in woods near the village of Montignac in France.
The discovery:	Caves containing over 2000 prehistoric paintings and engravings.

TIMELINE: INVENTION OF POTTERY

13,000 BC
The first potters discover they can make useful containers by shaping soft clay by hand then heating it in a fire to bake it hard.

6500 BC
Thin layers of coloured clay, called 'slip', and natural pigments, such as red ochre, are used to decorate pottery. Examples of this innovation have been found in the ancient city of Catal Huyuk (now Cumra in Turkey).

4000 - 3000 BC
The potter's wheel is invented. Mesopotamian potters use a slowly spinning stone wheel to produce pots with a uniform shape.

A Mesopotamian vase from around 3400 BC.

PAPYRUS PAPER

The ancient Egyptians invented papyrus, a type of paper made from papyrus reeds which grew by the River Nile.

Fibres from the reeds were squashed together into flat sheets. Then the sheets were dried in the sun.

A papyrus reed

INVENTION TIMELINE

c 4000 BC – Scales
Simple scales (a length of wood or metal balanced with pans hung from each end) are developed in Mesopotamia.

c 4000 BC – Gold/silver
Gold and silver are discovered. They are used for making ornaments and as a means of exchange.

c 3500 BC – Bricks
In the Middle East bricks are made from clay, then fired in a kiln to make them hard and waterproof. Prior to this bricks were made from mud and straw, but they sometimes dissolved in heavy rain!

c 3000 BC– Cotton
Cotton fabric is invented when the people of the Indus Valley (modern-day Pakistan) discover that the fibres attached to the cotton plant seeds can be woven into a fine fabric.

c 2600 BC – Chairs
The ancient Egyptians use chairs with padded seats and four legs. Ancient people had probably used many objects to sit on before this time, but chairs as we recognise them today were found in ancient Egyptian tombs from this period.

C 2500 BC – Ink/mirrors
Ink for writing is made from soot mixed with glue.

Mirrors made from discs of polished bronze or copper are used in ancient Egypt.

c 2000 BC – Wheel spokes
Mesopotamian craftsmen begin to produce wheels with a rim, hub and spokes instead of the heavy, solid plank-wheels previously used.

c 1500 BC – Flags
Flags are invented in China and used in battles. If a leader's flag is captured by his enemy, it means the enemy has won the battle.

c 600 BC – Rotary querns
The rotary quern is invented. For over 4000 years corn has been ground by hand using two stones. The rotary quern comprises a circular stone which fits into a stone base. The top stone is turned by a wooden handle crushing the grain between the two stones.

NATURAL WORLD

Humans have always wanted to know more about their origins and the Earth on which they live. Today, we know our planet is 4.5 billion years old, not the 74,832 years proposed by the French scientist Buffon in 1778. Palaeontologists have identified the first animals that lived on Earth and anthropologists have studied the fossils of our earliest ancestors. Scientists have discovered that all plants and animals are made from tiny building blocks called cells, and we now know that DNA within our cells makes us who we are.

Fossil hunter
William Buckland
(1784–1856)

DISCOVERING THE DINOSAURS

DINOSAUR FOSSILS
- In the 1820s, Englishwoman Mary Anning began a career as a professional fossil collector on the shores of Lyme Regis in England. Anning supplied the greatest scientists of the period with their material and during her career discovered fossils of *Plesiosaurs*, *Ichthyosaurs* and the first *Pterosaur* in Britain.

This illustration of an *Ichthyosaur* is based on fossil finds.

A *Megalosaurus* jawbone

THE FIRST DINOSAUR
- Fossils of a jawbone and teeth were found in Oxfordshire, England, in around 1815.

- William Buckland, of Oxford University, studied the fossils which he deduced were from a large, meat-eating reptile.

- In 1822, Buckland's colleague James Parkinson named the creature *Megalosaurus* (big lizard).

INVENTING DINOSAURS
- In 1842, English scientist Sir Richard Owen invented the term *'dinosauria'* to describe the *Megalosaurus* and two other fossil animals, *Iguanodon* and *Hylaeosaurus*, found at the time.

THE FIRST BIRD
In 1860, 1861 and 1877 the fossils of a single feather and of two birds were discovered in the same Jurassic limestone quarry in Solnhofen, Germany. The bird was named *Archaeopteryx*. It seemed to be a transition form between dinosaurs and birds.

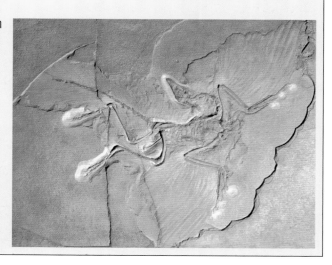

An *Archaeopteryx* fossil

CHARLES DARWIN

- During an expedition, English scientist Charles Darwin (1809-1882) was intrigued by the variety of bird species he observed in the Galapagos Islands.

- When, in 1837, ornithologist John Gould showed that, despite their differences, the Islands' birds were all closely related finches, it led Darwin to suggest that the various forms had evolved from a single species.

- In 1859, Darwin published *On the Origin of Species* a book presenting the theory that animals and plants have not always looked the way they do today, but have evolved from earlier forms, and are still evolving.

HOMO ERECTUS

The discovery:
The remains of a skull cap and some teeth with features similar to those of both apes and humans. Found in caves in Java (Indonesia). Nicknamed *'Java man'*.

Discovered by:
Dutch palaeontologist, Eugene Dubois in 1891.

Homo erectus skull

Discovery fact:
The first known fossils to be discovered of homo erectus.

- See page 10 discovery of LUCY (1974)

CONTINENTAL DRIFT

- In 1912, German meteorologist Alfred Wegener proposed that the world's continents were once joined together in a single, large landmass he called *'Pangaea'*.

- Over millions of years, the individual continents had drifted apart, but it is still possible to see how they fitted together.

Africa

South America

- Wegener's discovery of 'continental drift' was finally accepted by the world's scientists in the 1960s.

TIMELINE

1902 – Chromosomes
American surgeon Walter Sutton discovers the 'chromosome theory of inheritance'. He deduces that Mendel's features were controlled in living cells by structures called chromosomes. The chemical messages encoded in the chromosomes are the genes.

1909 – Burgess Shale
American palaeontologist Charles Walcott discovers the Burgess Shale fossil site in Canada's Rocky Mountains. Dating from the Cambrian period it contains thousands of fossils of marine animals.

1927 – Birth of a universe
Belgian priest Georges Lemaitre proposes a forerunner of the Big Bang theory: that the universe began with the explosion of a primeval atom.

1953 – Age of the Earth
Fiesel Houtermans and Claire Patterson use radiometric dating to date the Earth at 4.5 billion years.

1963 – Plate tectonics
Fred Vine and Drummond Matthews discover seafloor spreading. This leads to the understanding of plate tectonics.

1964 – The Big Bang
Arno Penzias and Robert Wilson detect cosmic radiation (radiation coming from space) and use it to confirm the 'Big Bang Theory'.

1980 – Dinosaur extinction
Luis and Walter Alvarez put forward the asteroid impact theory of dinosaur extinction.

1985 – Ozone depletion
Scientists of the British Antarctic Survey discover the depletion of ozone in the upper atmosphere.

1991 – Asteroid impact
Chicxulub crater in Yucatán is pinpointed as the site of the asteroid impact which caused the extinction of the dinosaurs.

- See the GLOSSARY for explanations of many of the scientific terms used in this timeline.

THE STORY OF DNA

1869 - DNA discovered
Swiss graduate chemist Johann Miescher identifies a particular substance – deoxyribonucleic acid (DNA) – in the nuclei of white blood cells. The importance of this discovery goes unnoticed for more than 50 years.

1929 - DNA molecule
In the USA, Russian-born chemist Phoebus Levene establishes that the DNA molecule is composed of a series of nucleotides each composed of a sugar, a phosphate group and one of four bases: thymine (T), guanine (G), cytosine (C), adenine (A).

1950 - Base pairs
In the USA, biochemist Erwin Chargaff discovers that the bases are arranged in pairs, and that the composition of DNA is identical within species, but differs between species.

1952 - The genetic code
Two American scientists, Alfred Hershey and Martha Chase, conduct an experiment proving that the DNA molecule is the means by which genetic information is transmitted.

1952 - DNA analysis
In England, scientists Maurice Wilkins and Rosalind Franklin analyse the DNA molecule using X-rays.

1953 - The shape of DNA
Wilkins' and Franklin's results enable the shape of the DNA molecule to be determined by Crick and Watson.

1965 - Cell proteins
American biochemist Marshall Nirenberg deciphers the genetic code through which DNA controls the production of proteins inside body cells

1983 - Polymerase chain reaction
American researcher Kary Mullis invents the polymerase chain reaction (PCR), a laboratory process that enables scientists to duplicate small sections of the DNA molecule many millions of times in a short period of time.

- See page 51 FRANCIS CRICK AND JAMES WATSON.
- See the GLOSSARY for scientific terms used in this timeline.

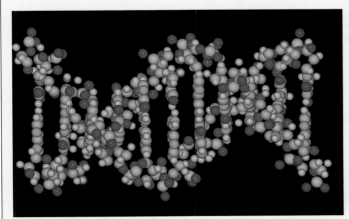

A DNA molecule

SCIENCE ALL AROUND

Science is simply the close observation of nature. Although many scientists now use sophisticated equipment such as lasers and hadron colliders, their basic technique is the same as taught in every school science class: observe, investigate, understand and describe. Potential new discoveries are all around us. For example, an amazing new form of carbon, that scientists had previously thought impossible, was recently discovered in some residue that had built up around an old electric lamp!

• See page 12
DISCOVERING AND INVENTING METAL.

THE PERIODIC TABLE

In 1869, Russian chemist Dmitri Mendeleyev discovered that the elements can be placed in ascending sequence of atomic size, arranged across a periodic table of rows and columns. Elements with similar physical or chemical properties are located near to each other.

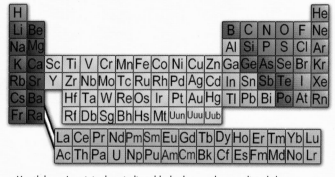

Mendeleyev's original periodic table had gaps that predicted the existence of undiscovered elements. These gaps have since been filled.

THE INVENTION OF THE MICROSCOPE

THE FIRST MICROSCOPE
The first working microscope was constructed in the Netherlands in 1668 by Anton van Leeuwenhoek.

It had a small convex (bean-shaped) lens and could magnify around 200 times. The entire instrument was only 10 cm long. The user held it up to the eye.

DISCOVERING BACTERIA
In 1674, van Leeuwenhoek was the first person to observe protozoa (from ponds). In 1676, he examined bacteria from his own mouth.

VAN LEEUWENHOEK'S MICROSCOPE

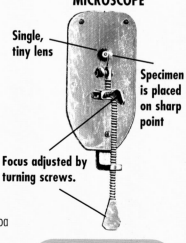

Single, tiny lens

Specimen is placed on sharp point

Focus adjusted by turning screws.

• See page 53
INVENTORS AT WORK for more microscope inventions.

A NEW CARBON

In 1985, three university professors jointly discovered an exciting new form of the carbon molecule.

Instead of just four atoms like other forms of carbon, it has 60 atoms arranged in a hollow, multi-sided, geometric shape.

The new substance, which is incredibly strong for its weight, has been named *buckminsterfullerene* and the hollow shapes are known as *buckyballs*.

HIGH ENERGY COLLISIONS

To study the structure of atoms, scientists build massive devices that use magnetism to accelerate bits of atomic nuclei so that they crash into each other at very high speeds and break apart.

The first such device, called a *cyclotron*, was built in the USA in 1933. The latest device, known as a *Large Hadron Collider*, is located on the border between France and Switzerland.

LASERS

THE FIRST LASER
In 1960, scientist Theodore Maiman built the first laser (Light Amplification by Stimulated Emission of Radiation). It used a rod-shaped crystal of synthetic ruby to produce a very bright, very narrow beam of light.

Gas lasers were invented a few months after the ruby laser.

WHAT IS A LASER?
In a laser, a crystal or gas is energised so that its atoms start to emit light. The light produced by a laser is of nearly uniform wavelength and the light rays are almost perfectly parallel so that there is very little spreading of the beam.

An experiment showing an intense ruby laser beam penetrating two prisms.

LASER BEAMS ON THE MOON
In the 1970s, lasers were used to measure the exact distance between the Earth and the Moon. The narrow beam of a laser was bounced off reflectors which had been put on the moon's surface by Apollo astronauts.

LASERS ALL AROUND
Today, tiny semiconductor devices, smaller than a pinhead, produce the laser light that reads the digital information encoded onto CDs and DVDs.

THE STORY OF GENETIC ENGINEERING

- See page 14 TIMELINE for Gregor Mendel's discovery of heredity.

1954 - GENETIC CODE
Russian physicist George Gamow is the first to suggest that the DNA bases T, G, C and A form a genetic code that looks like: CGCTGACATCGT etc.

1966 - FROG CLONING
In England, biologist John Gurdon clones frogs from cells taken from the intestines of a tadpole.

1971 - RESTRICTION ENZYMES
In the USA, molecular biologists Daniel Nathans and Hamilton Smith discover restriction enzymes that can be used to cut the DNA molecule into short strands.

1972 - RECOMBINANT DNA
American scientist Patrick Berg succeeds in splicing together strands of DNA to produce recombinant DNA (DNA that has been recombined from a number of different strands) this marks the beginning of true genetic engineering.

1994 - GM CROPS
In the USA, a rot-resistant tomato becomes the first genetically modified (GM) crop to be approved for sale to the public.

1996 - A CLONED MAMMAL
In Scotland, a team of scientists led by Ian Wilmut succeed in producing Dolly the sheep, the world's first cloned mammal.

Dolly the cloned sheep had no immediate practical value, but the cloning technique is vital. If, for example, scientists can genetically engineer a cow to produce milk that contains life-saving drugs, then they can use the cloning technique to make thousands of identical cows.

- See page 15 THE STORY OF DNA.
- See the GLOSSARY for scientific terms used in this timeline.

MAKING DOLLY THE SHEEP
- The nucleus was removed from an unfertilised egg.
- Next, a cell from an adult sheep was fused with the egg by passing an electric current through the two.
- They became one cell which then behaved like a fertilised egg and began to divide.
- Finally, the cell was implanted into another female sheep where it developed normally into an embryo.

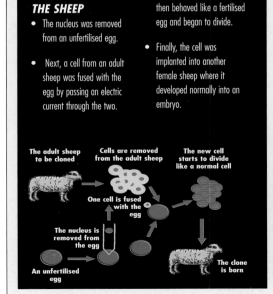

The adult sheep to be cloned

Cells are removed from the adult sheep

The new cell starts to divide like a normal cell

One cell is fused with the egg

The nucleus is removed from the egg

An unfertilised egg

The clone is born

Dr. Ian Wilmut with Dolly the sheep.

ELECTRICITY TIMELINE

1800 – First battery
Italian physicist Alessandro Volta invents the first electric battery. It uses chemical reactions to produce electric current.

1807 – Electrolysis
English scientist Humphry Davy invents the process of extracting metals from minerals by electrolysis. He heats the minerals to melting point and then applies an electric current.

1820 – Ampere's Law
French scientist Andre Ampere experiments with magnets and electricity and discovers the mathematical relationship (Ampere's Law) between magnetism and the flow of electrical current.

1827 – Ohm's law
In Germany, the physicist Georg Ohm discovers the relationship (Ohm's law) between resistance and current in an electrical circuit.

1831 – Induction
English scientist Michael Faraday discovers the laws of induction that explain how a variable magnetic field causes electrical current to flow through copper wires – the principle behind both the electric generator and the electric motor.

1864 – Electricity and magnetism
Scottish mathematician James Maxwell discovers four basic equations that describe all the relationships between electricity and magnetism.

1888 – First generator
Croatian inventor Nikola Tesla designs the world's first successful alternating current (AC) generator. Alternating current (used for mains electricity) is more powerful than the direct current (DC) produced by batteries.

1947 – The transistor
In America, electrical engineers invent the transistor, the world's first semiconductor device, marking the start of the 'Electronic Age'.

- See the GLOSSARY for a detailed definition of a SEMICONDUCTOR.

EXPLORING SPACE

The first skywatchers looked to the heavens and asked questions about the planets and stars they could see. When the telescope was invented in the 17th century, astronomers were finally able to study the stars and the planets in more detail. In the early 20th Century, pioneering rocket scientists such as Konstantin Tsiolkovsky, Robert Goddard, Herman Oberth and Werner von Braun expanded our horizons further when they developed the means to blast a satellite, or a man, into space.

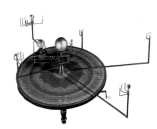

The orrery, a mechanical model of our solar system, invented in the mid 1700s.

1543 – Sun-centred universe
Polish astronomer Copernicus publishes his 'Six Books Concerning the Revolutions of the Heavenly Orbs' presenting his discoveries and his theory of a universe with the Sun at the centre.

1609 – Galileo's telescope
Galileo hears of Lippershey's invention and builds his own telescope. He uses his new instrument to make many discoveries, including Jupiter's four largest moons and sunspots from which he deduces that the Sun rotates.

1610 – Orion Nebula
Frenchman Nicolas-Claude Fabri de Peiresc discovers the Orion Nebula (or Great Nebula). This star 'nursery' is visible with the naked eye. Stars are being born there right now.

1705 – Halley's Comet
Edmond Halley discovers that comets observed in 1531, 1607 and 1682 are the same comet. He predicts the comet will return in 1758. The comet is sighted in that year (after Halley's death) and named in his honour.

1922-1924 – New galaxies
American astronomer Edwin Hubble discovers that there are other galaxies outside of the Milky Way.

1931 – Radio waves from space
American engineer Karl Jansky is assigned by Bell Telephone Laboratories, New Jersey, USA, to track down interference which is causing problems to telephone communications. Jansky finds all the sources except one. In 1931, after months of study, he establishes that the radio interference is coming from the stars.

1995 – Comet Hale-Bopp
US amateur astronomers Alan Hale, in New Mexico, and Thomas Bopp, in Arizona, independently discover a new comet on 23 July, 1995. At its brightest in 1997, Hale-Bopp was a thousand times brighter than Halley's comet.

ROCKET PIONEERS

1150 – Chinese rockets
Gunpowder propelled rockets are invented by the Chinese.

c1900 – Tsiolkovsky
Russian scientist Konstantin Tsiolkovsky suggests using rockets with stages that can be jettisoned to get large objects into space.

1926 – Goddard's Rocket
American Robert Goddard experiments with different fuels. In 1926, the first rocket to use a liquid propellant was launched from Goddard's Aunt Effie's cabbage patch.

Goddard's work earned him the title the *Father of modern rocketry*.

1920s – 1930s
German Herman Oberth develops much of the modern theory for rocket and spaceflight. German scientist Werner von Braun, produces the V2 rocket (a weapon) for Germany in WWII, then goes to America to work on the space programme.

INVENTION OF THE TELESCOPE

HANS LIPPERSHEY
Dutch spectacle-maker Hans Lippershey is credited with inventing the refracting telescope in 1608. Lippershey discovered that if you look through two lenses of the right type, they will enlarge distant objects.

Lippershey offered his new 'looker' to the government for use in warfare, and was granted 900 florins for the instrument, but there was a requirement that it be modified into a binocular device.

REFRACTING TELESCOPES
Refracting telescopes (below) work by having a convex lens which bends light rays from an object to form an upside-down image of the object. A second lens, the eyepiece, bends the rays again and magnifies the image.

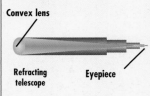

Convex lens

Refracting telescope

Eyepiece

Newton's telescope

NEWTON'S TELESCOPE
In 1668, English mathematician Isaac Newton developed the reflecting telescope. English astronomer John Gregory had thought up an alternative reflector design in 1663.

REFLECTING TELESCOPES
A reflecting telescope (below) uses a shaped primary mirror to reflect light to a smaller secondary mirror. The light is then reflected to the focus and the image is viewed through an eyepiece.

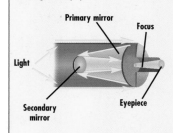

Primary mirror

Focus

Light

Secondary mirror

Eyepiece

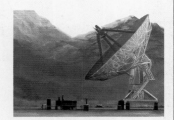

RADIO TELESCOPES
Radio telescopes receive the radio waves emitted by objects in space and, via a computer, convert those waves to images.

Radio waves can penetrate through dust clouds that block visible light.

See page 18 TIMELINE RADIO WAVES FROM SPACE.

Some of the planets in our Solar System have been known for many years, others were discovered more recently. Both astronomers on Earth and space probes have added to the long list of solar system discoveries.

JUPITER

Jupiter's 'Great Red Spot' (GRS) was discovered by the French astronomer, Gian Domenico Cassini in 1665 using an early telescope.

Thanks to space probes we now know the GRS measures around 12,000 km by 25,000 km and is a vast, violent storm.

VENUS

Following the mapping of Venus's surface by NASA's Magellan probe (1990–1994), scientists discovered that Venus is covered in volcanoes, including an active volcano Maat Mons. Venus and Earth are the only two planets known to have active volcanoes.

MERCURY

When Mercury was first photographed by the NASA probe Mariner 10 in 1974, it was discovered that Mercury has many deep craters. The largest, the Caloris Basin, is around 1300 km across.

PLUTO

Pluto's existence had been predicted by astronomer Percival Lowell, but it was actually discovered by American Clyde Tombaugh at the Lowell Observatory in 1930.

In 1978, Pluto's close satellite, Charon, was discovered by James Walter Christy.

URANUS

Sir William Herschel discovered Uranus on 13 March, 1781, using a home-made reflecting telescope that was 2 metres long. Herschel originally thought Uranus was a comet.

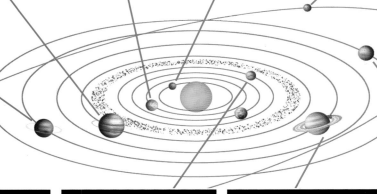

Pluto

Charon

NEPTUNE

Neptune was discovered in 1846 by astronomer J.G. Gale in Berlin. Neptune's position had been predicted by mathematicians John Couch Adams in England and Urbain Le Verrier in France.

MARS - CRATERS

In 1971, the space probe Mariner 9 discovered a system of canyons known as the Valles Marineris. The canyons stretch for around 4000 km. Some individual canyons are 100 km wide and some are 8 to 10 km deep.

MARS

The largest volcano in the Solar System, Olympus Mons, was discovered on Mars. It is 27 km high. The tallest volcano on Earth, Mauna Loa in Hawaii, rises 9 km above the ocean floor.

SATURN

Saturn's ring system was discovered by Galileo in 1610. Galileo's primitive telescope could not make out the structure of the rings. We now know that the rings are made of millions of small chunks of rock and ice.

IT CAME FROM SPACE

We all benefit from inventions developed by NASA for space missions.

- Battery-powered tools were invented for use in space where there are no electrical sockets.

- The digital watch was invented to help astronauts keep accurate time.

- Plastic sandwich boxes were originally used to keep food for astronauts fresh.

MARS - MOONS

In 1877, the American astronomer Asaph Hall discovered Mars's two moons. He named them Phobos and Deimos after the sons of Ares, the Greek counterpart of the Roman god Mars.

This is the rod-like structure which some scientists believe to be a fossilised, microscopic Martian creature.

HUBBLE SPACE TELESCOPE

The Hubble Space Telescope is a satellite built by NASA and ESA. It was launched in 1990 and orbits the Earth at around 600 km above Earth's surface.

- The telescope is named after astronomer Edwin Hubble.

- Hubble is a reflecting telescope, and it also works in ultraviolet. It is powered by two solar panels.

- Hubble is designed to look a long way beyond the solar system. The volume of space it can cover is 350 times bigger than can be seen from the Earth.

LIFE ON MARS

In 1996, US geologist David S. McKay and a team from NASA's Johnson Space Center, in Houston, reported that they had found evidence of microscopic life on Mars. The tiny microbes were found inside a meteorite which had travelled from Mars to Earth possibly taking millions of years. At present, many scientists do not agree with McKay's findings.

• See page 15 THE STORY OF DNA.
• See page 17 THE STORY OF GENETIC ENGINEERING.

Most body activities, including how we move or digest food, are now well understood thanks to discoveries made in the past 500 years. The earliest anatomists studied the structure of body organs such as the heart and kidneys. Later, physiologists discovered how these organs worked. Today, there are still things to learn. *The Human Genome Project* for example, having 'read' the DNA in our cells, is now identifying the instructions needed to build and run a human being.

Anatomist Andreas Vesalius (1514–1564)

TIMELINE: BLOOD DISCOVERIES

1628 - Blood circulation
British doctor William Harvey proves through experiments that blood circulates around the body, pumped by the heart along blood vessels.

1658 - Red blood cells
Red blood cells are first observed and identified by Dutch naturalist Jan Swammerdam using an early microscope.

1661 - Blood capillaries
The existence of blood capillaries (tiny blood vessels that link arteries to veins) is discovered by Italian microscopist Marcello Malpighi.

1884 - Action of white blood cells
Russian zoologist Elie Metchnikoff describes how white blood cells surround and devour bacteria and other germs.

1901 - Blood groups
The existence of blood groups is discovered by Austrian-American doctor Karl Landsteiner. The four blood groups are later named A, B, AB and O. Blood transfusions will only work if the right type of blood is given, so Landsteiner's discoveries pave the way for safe blood transfusions.

1959 - Haemoglobin structure
Scientist Max Perutz discovers the structure of haemoglobin, the substance inside red blood cells that carries oxygen and makes the cells red.

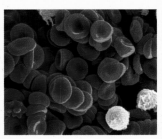

Blood cells

THE HUMAN GENOME PROJECT

• In the late 1980s, groups of scientists around the world set out on an unprecedented research project – to produce a map of the human genome, or human genetic code.

• Several anonymous donors provided DNA for the project. The resulting DNA map will be typical of all human DNA.

• In 2000, scientists released a 'rough draft' of the human genome showing all of the 3 billion or so base pairs in human DNA.

• In April 2003, *The Human Genome Project* completed the map, giving scientists the ability, for the first time, to read nature's complete genetic blueprint for building a human.

• It will take decades to understand what all the 25,000 to 30,000 human genes do, but scientists hope that new treatments and earlier diagnosis of diseases will be among the many benefits of this vast and pioneering project.

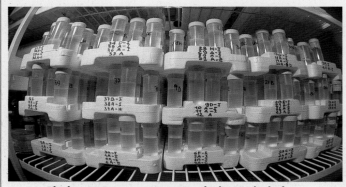

Phials containing every gene in the human body from the Human Genome Project.

• See the GLOSSARY for explanations of many of the scientific terms used in this timeline.

The human body is made up of 100 trillion cells of 200 different types. It has taken hundreds of years to understand how it works, and there are still more discoveries to be made.

EAR

The ear was first described in detail by Italian anatomist Bartolomeo Eustachio in 1562. He gave his name to the eustachian tube that connects the air-filled middle ear to the back of the throat.

BRAIN

Part of the left side of the brain, called Broca's area, controls speech. It was first described in 1861 by French doctor Pierre Paul Broca. He made his discovery while treating a brain-damaged patient.

PITUITARY GLAND

In 1912, American doctor Harvey Cushing described the pituitary gland and how it works. This raisin-sized gland, at the base of the brain, is vitally important, releasing nine hormones that control growth, reproduction and many other body activities.

VEINS

Veins are blood vessels that return blood to the heart. In 1603, Italian anatomist Hieronymus Fabricius showed that veins have valves. These prevent the backflow of blood away from the heart.

LUNGS

In the 1600s, British doctor John Mayow discovered that 'breathing in' happens when the chest gets bigger making the lungs expand to suck in air. He experimented with models of the chest made from bellows.

PANCREAS

Made and released by the pancreas, the hormone insulin controls levels of glucose in the blood. Insulin was first isolated in 1921 by Canadian scientists Frederick Banting and Charles Best.

KIDNEYS

In 1842, British doctor William Bowman described the microscopic structure of the kidney. Two years later, in 1844, German scientist Karl Ludwig discovered how the kidneys make urine.

STOMACH

Digestion in the stomach was first described in 1833 by American doctor William Beaumont. He experimented by dangling food into a man's stomach through a hole in his side produced by a shooting accident.

LIVER

In the 1850's, French physiologist Claude Bernard was the first person to investigate what the liver, the body's largest internal organ, does. We now know the liver performs over 500 vital functions.

FEMALE REPRODUCTIVE SYSTEM

In 1672, this system was described in detail by Dutch anatomist Regnier de Graaf. Earlier, in 1561, Italian anatomist Gabriello Fallopio described the fallopian tube that links the ovary to the uterus.

MUSCLES

How muscles contract (get shorter) to pull bones and move the body was discovered independently in 1954 by British scientists Andrew Huxley and Hugh Huxley.

BONE

Bones are hard and strong because they contain rigid, microscopic cylinders that lie in parallel to each other. These are named Haversian systems after Clopton Havers, a British doctor who described bone structure in 1691.

1796 – Vaccination
Edward Jenner performs the first vaccination against smallpox.

1851 – Ophthalmoscope
German scientist Hermann von Helmholtz invents the ophthalmoscope, a device for looking into and examining the inside of the eye.

1867 – Thermometer
English doctor Thomas Allbutt devises the first accurate clinical thermometer for measuring body temperature.

1882 – Tuberculosis
German doctor Robert Koch discovers bacterium that causes the disease tuberculosis (TB).

1895 – X-rays
German physicist Wilhelm Roentgen discovers X-rays.

1896 – Sphygmomanometer
Italian doctor Scipione Riva-Rocci devises the first accurate sphygmomanometer, a device for measuring blood pressure.

1903 – Electrocardiograph
Dutch scientist Willem Einthoven devises the electrocardiograph (ECG), a machine that monitors heart beats.

1910 – Salvarsan
German scientist Paul Ehrlich discovers salvarsan. It is used to treat syphilis and is the first drug to treat a specific disease.

1928 – Penicillin
Alexander Fleming discovers the antibiotic penicillin.

1943 – Kidney dialysis
Dutch doctor Willem Kolff invents the dialysis machine to treat people with kidney failure.

1958 – Ultrasound images
Ultrasound is used for the first time to produce images of a fetus in its mother's uterus.

• See page 15
THE STORY OF DNA.
• See page 17 THE STORY OF
GENETIC ENGINEERING.

MEDICINE

A disease, or illness stops your body working normally. Medicine involves finding out how a disease can be cured or prevented. Advances in medicine mean that today's doctors can diagnose and treat many illnesses. Hi-tech methods such as CT scans allow doctors to look inside a living body for possible problems, while modern surgery removes, repairs or replaces damaged body parts. Drugs, such as the germ-killing antibiotic penicillin, are being developed all the time to combat specific diseases.

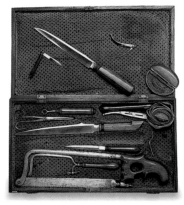

An 18th century case of surgical instruments. Many of the implements were used for amputations – a common remedy when little was know about bacterial infections.

THE STETHOSCOPE

In 1819, French doctor René Laënnec invented the stethoscope, an instrument used by doctors to listen to a patient's breathing and heart rate.
Since 1819, Laënnec's *cylindre*, a wooden tube, has been improved many times to produce the instrument used today.

ANTISEPTIC SURGERY

Joseph Lister was a British surgeon and the founder of antiseptic surgery.

• In 1867, Lister introduced dressings soaked in carbolic acid and strict rules of hygiene to kill bacteria.

• Lister's methods increased the survival rate from surgery dramatically. Prior to this, around half of all surgical patients died from gangrene or secondary infections.

Joseph Lister

ALEXANDER FLEMING 1881 – 1955

Sir Alexander Fleming at a microscope in his laboratory at St. Mary's Hospital, London (c1929).

Nationality: Scottish

Profession: Bacteriologist

Biographical information: Fleming trained as a doctor at St Mary's Hospital, London, and served in the Medical Corps during World War I. He became interested in the problem of controlling infections caused by bacteria and continued his research after the war.

Most famous discovery: Fleming discovered penicillin, the first antibiotic. Antibiotics are drugs that kill bacteria. They are now used to treat many illnesses and diseases.

Eureka moment: One morning in 1928, Fleming was preparing a routine set of bacteria cultures when he noticed that something was killing the bacteria. When he investigated, he found that it was a bread mould called penicillin.

Scientists at work: Two other scientists, Howard Florey and Ernst Chain, helped perfect the manufacture of penicillin, and they shared the 1945 *Nobel Prize for Medicine* with Fleming.

DISCOVERING X-RAYS

WILHELM ROENTGEN

In November 1895, German physicist Wilhelm Roentgen found that by passing electricity through a vacuum he produced a new type of high energy radiation that he called X (for unknown) rays.

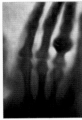

SEEING BONES

An X-ray of Roentgen's wife's hand (1895).

Roentgen also discovered that a beam of X-rays could pass through the body to produce an image on a photographic plate. Roentgen found that while bones appeared as clear images on the plate, soft tissues, such as muscle and skin, were much less distinct.

LOOKING INSIDE THE BODY

Within weeks, Roentgen's discovery was greeted as one of the most significant in the history of medicine. For the first time doctors could look inside the living body without having to cut it open. Today X-rays are used routinely to detect broken bones and other disorders.

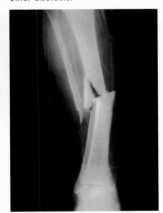

An X-ray showing a broken leg bone.

CT SCANNERS

X-rays are also used in combination with computers in Computed Tomography Scanners. CT scanners produce images in the form of body 'slices' that show both hard and soft tissues. The idea of CT scanners was first developed by British engineer Godfrey Hounsfield in 1967.

TIMELINE: FIRST TEST-TUBE BABY

British biologist Robert Edwards and British gynaecologist Patrick Steptoe developed IVF (in vitro fertilisation) as a way to help infertile women have babies.

Patrick Steptoe (left) and Robert Edwards.

1966
Edwards and Steptoe remove ripe eggs from women's' ovaries and fertilise them with sperm outside of the body.

1972
Edwards and Steptoe place eggs, fertilised in the laboratory, back inside the bodies of women with damaged fallopian tubes, hoping the eggs will implant. They make more than 80 unsuccessful attempts.

1977
British couple Lesley and John Brown begin IVF treatment. Lesley Brown conceives.

1978
Louise Joy Brown, the first test-tube baby is born 25 July, 1978.

SURGICAL TIMELINE

1770s – Art of surgery
English doctor John Hunter transforms surgery (the process of cutting into the body to treat disease) from a lowly craft to a progressive medical science.

1846 – Anaesthetic
The first public demonstration of ether anaesthetic is carried out by anaesthetist William Morton during a surgical operation in Boston, USA.

1865-1867 – Antiseptic surgery
Joseph Lister pioneers use of germ-killing antiseptic during operations.

1937 – Hip replacement
In London, surgeon Philip Wiles performs the first hip replacement surgery using a stainless steel 'ball and socket'.

1940 – Plastic surgery
The first skin grafts, to repair burns suffered by WWII pilots, are carried out by English surgeon Archibald McIndoe.

1944 – Cardiac surgery
A pioneering operation by American doctors Alfred Blalock and Helen Taussig, to treat heart disease in babies, establishes the specialty of cardiac (heart) surgery.

1954 – Kidney transplant
The first successful kidney transplant operation (transferring a healthy kidney from a donor to a recipient with a diseased kidney) is carried out in Boston, USA.

1967 – Heart transplant
The first heart transplant operation is carried out by South African surgeon Christiaan Barnard.

1969 – Microsurgery
First use, in USA, of microsurgery in which a surgeon uses a binocular microscope to magnify tiny blood vessels or nerves while she/he repairs them.

1980 – Keyhole surgery
The introduction of 'keyhole' surgery, which is carried out through small incisions in the skin.

1987 – Laser eye surgery
In America, laser eye surgery (which uses intense heat to repair damaged tissues) is first performed.

2002 – Surgical robots
First robot-assisted cardiac operation in the USA.

EDWARD JENNER 1749 – 1823

Nationality: British
Profession: Doctor
Biographical information: Edward Jenner was born in the village of Berkeley, in England. He trained as a surgeon before studying medicine in London. He returned home as a doctor in 1773.
Most famous discovery:
The discovery and initial

development of vaccination.

Eureka moment: Milkmaid Sarah Nelmes boasted that she could not catch smallpox because she had earlier caught the less serious disease cowpox from the cows she milked. A smallpox outbreak in 1788 proved that she was right. All of Jenner's patients who had caught

cowpox did not get smallpox.

Scientist at work: In 1796, Jenner proved his theory by infecting a small boy first with cowpox and then with smallpox. He found that the boy was immune to the disease. Jenner called his treatment vaccination (from the Latin word for cowpox – *vaccina*).

EARLY INDUSTRY

• See page 35 for
FASHION INVENTIONS.

The process that we call the *Industrial Revolution* spread across three centuries and was the result of countless inventions, developments and improvements. Two key factors were the widespread availability of metals, especially iron and steel, and the introduction of machinery. The textile industry was the first to be affected by the Industrial Revolution and the first modern factories for spinning cotton were built in the 18th century in northern England.

The Spinning Jenny

THE JACQUARD LOOM

• The first programmable machine was Joseph-Marie Jacquard's loom.

• The pattern woven by the loom was controlled by cards with holes punched in them. Changing the pattern of holes, changed the pattern woven into the cloth.

MUNTZ METAL

In 1832, English businessman George Muntz invented an alloy of copper (60%) and zinc (40%), it was known as Muntz metal. This new alloy soon replaced pure copper for sheathing the hulls of wooden ships.

MASS PRODUCTION

Mass production depends on three things: the use of machinery, interchangeable components, and the assembly line.

MADE BY HAND
The first machines were individually made by hand. The idea of interchangeable parts was first introduced in France, in 1785, for making the firing mechanisms of sporting guns.

MANUFACTURING FIREARMS
In 1801, inventor Eli Whitney demonstrated for the US government his system of interchangeable parts for the manufacture of military firearms.

SAMUEL COLT
In 1855, American industrialist Samuel Colt set up a factory that used interchangeable parts and a production line to make handguns of his own design.

RANSOM OLDS
In1901, in the USA, inventor Ransom Olds introduced production line methods into the newly established automobile industry for the manufacture of his Oldsmobile buggy.

MODEL T PRODUCTION LINE
In 1913, American industrialist Henry Ford built the world's first fully integrated factory assembly line for the production of the famous Model T Ford.

Workers added parts to cars as the cars moved by. The man hours required to build a car dropped from 12 hours to 1.5 hours. A car was produced every 24 seconds.

• See page 26
HENRY FORD.

A line of Model T chassis. The car bodies were manufactured on the upper floor of the factory then lowered onto the chassis which were built on the lower floor.

THE CONSTRUCTION INDUSTRY

FIRST IRON BRIDGE
In 1777, the world's first iron bridge was constructed across the River Severn at Coalbrookdale in Shropshire, England.

PRE-FABRICATED BUILDING
In 1851, *The Crystal Palace* was built entirely from iron and glass to accommodate the Great Exhibition in London, England. Engineer and botanist Joseph Paxton designed the building, based on the design of plant glasshouses. Paxton's revolutionary design contained over 300,000 panes of glass and hundreds of ready-made, cast-iron frames that simply bolted together on site – an instant building!

REINFORCED CONCRETE
In 1867, in France, amateur inventor Joseph Monier made the first successful reinforced concrete using lateral iron rods.

The Crystal Palace under construction. Six million people visited the Great Exhibition to see the best of British industry, from steam trains to spinning machines.

IRON BUILDINGS
In 1889, the Eiffel Tower in Paris, France, was the last major building to be made from iron – in the future, steel would be used instead.

STEEL-FRAMED SKYSCRAPER
By the second half of the 19th century, business space in US cities was much in demand. The refinement of the Bessemer steel-making process (1855) made it possible to construct very high buildings because steel is both stronger than iron, and lighter. The development of the first safety lift also made skyscrapers (buildings of 10 to 20 storeys high) possible.

PRE-STRESSED CONCRETE
In 1928, French Engineer Eugene Freyssinet was the first to make use of pre-stressed concrete.

DYNAMITE – AN EXPLOSIVE INVENTION

The invention: Dynamite – a type of nitro-glycerine explosive that could be handled safely. Dynamite became widely used in the mining and construction industries.
Invented: 1866
Invented by: Swedish chemist Alfred Nobel.
Other inventions: Blasting gelatin, smokeless powder for firearms, and explosives specifically for military purposes (although Nobel later developed a bad

conscience about this).
Inventor fact: When Nobel died in 1896, he bequeathed most of his fortune to establish *Nobel Prizes* for peace and scientific achievement.

OTIS SAFETY LIFT

- Elisha Otis worked in a US bed factory. Simple cargo lifts were used to move goods to upper floors. Otis invented a safety device which had arms that shot out from the lift car and grabbed the side of the lift shaft if the rope broke. To demonstrate his invention, he had the cable cut while he was in a lift at the World's Fair of 1853.

- Skyscrapers would not have been built were it not for Otis's invention.

FANTASTIC PLASTIC

Plastics replaced a range of traditional materials used in industry, such as wood, metal, glass, ceramics, natural fibres, ivory and bone.

PARKESINE
In 1862, the English chemist Alexander Parkes produced the world's first plastic, named Parkesine. The material could be squeezed into a mold while soft and was made into

small decorative items, such as hair slides.

CELLULOID
In the late 1860s, American inventor John Hyatt discovered how to make celluloid while looking for an ivory-substitute for making billiard balls. Celluloid was made into combs, piano keys, dolls, knife handles and film. However, it was highly flammable and caused many accidents.

BAKELITE
In 1910, the Belgian-born American chemist Leo Baekeland invented the first thermosetting plastic (a plastic that sets permanently when heated).

It was named Bakelite. Hard and chemically resistant, Bakelite is a nonconductor of electricity so it was used in all sorts of electrical appliances.

POLYCARBONATE
In 1953, Dr. Daniel Fox, a chemist at General Electric, created a gooey substance that hardened in a beaker. He found he could not break or destroy the material. LEXAN polycarbonate is now available in over 35,000 colours. PC has been used in vehicle windows, helmets worn by the first men on the moon, fighter jet windshields, laptop computer housings, CDs and DVDs.

IRON & STEEL TIMELINE

1709 – Quality iron
In England, Abraham Darby first produces good quality iron by smelting iron ore with coke (baked coal). Coke burns with a hotter flame than charcoal and can be used to fuel much larger furnaces.

1709 – Iron bars
In Sweden, the engineer Christopher Polhelm invents a grooved roller that can be used for making iron bars.

1750 – Crucible steel
In England, the clockmaker Benjamin Huntsman perfects a process for making steel by heating high-quality iron in a special reverbatory furnace. Called crucible steel, this new metal is so hard that knife makers at first refuse to use it.

1783 – Puddling process
The English ironmaker Henry Cort patents his 'puddling' process that converts the brittle 'pig iron', produced by smelting, into wrought iron which can be easily hammered and pressed into pots, pans and other household items.

1847 – Steel maker
The American iron maker William Kelly discovers that he can convert iron to steel by blasting jets of air onto molten iron.

1855 – Bessemer process
In England, the inventor Henry Bessemer patents his own method of making steel using blasts of air.

1864 – Siemens-Martin
The Martin iron works in France begins producing steel in an open-hearth furnace invented by the German engineer William Siemens. The Siemens-Martin process later becomes the world's leading method of steel production.

1866 – Air boiling
In the USA, Henry Kelly patents his 'air boiling' method of steel making.

1877 – Quality steel
In England, cousins Percy and Sidney Gilchrist invent a method of dephosphorizing steel to produce better quality metal.

- **See page 12 DISCOVERING AND INVENTING METAL.**

ENGINE POWER

ROAD VEHICLE TIMELINE

1838 – Pedal power
Kirkpatrick Macmillan, a Scottish blacksmith, invents the bicycle when he improves the recently invented 'dandy-horse' or 'velocipede'. He adds a pair of pedals that drive the rear wheel.

1881 – Electric vehicle
The world's first electric vehicle is driven around the streets of Paris, France. The electric power is supplied from storage batteries developed by Gaston Plante and Camille Faure.

1885 – Automobile
In Germany, the mechanical engineer Carl Benz builds and test-drives the world's first automobile, a tricycle powered by an internal combustion engine. Benz's motor tricycle has a top speed of 13 km/h.

1885 – Motorcycle
Gottlieb Daimler (who also invented the petrol engine) builds the world's first motorcycle in conjunction with the German inventor Wilhelm Maybach.

1888 – Pneumatic tyre
The Scottish veterinary surgeon John Dunlop patents the pneumatic tyre. He invented the tyre to give his son a more comfortable ride on his tricycle.

1904 – Commercial success
The four-wheel, curved-dash Oldsmobile designed by Ransom Olds becomes the world's first commercially successful automobile when some 4000 are sold in the USA in a single year.

1908 – Model T
American industrialist Henry Ford introduces the Model T – 'the car you can have in any colour, as long as it's black'. The Model T marks the true beginning of the automobile age.

• See page 24 MASS PRODUCTION.

For thousands of years people had to rely on muscle power for making overland journeys – they walked, rode on horseback or sat in a wagon pulled by draught animals. Beginning in the 18th century, the traditional forms of transport were transformed by the invention and development of new sources of mechanical power in the form of the steam engine, and later the internal combustion engine.

The blossoming film industry of the 1920s was quick to see the potential of the motor car – Ford's Model Ts were soon in the movies!

INVENTION OF THE ENGINE

An engine is a device for transforming heat from burned fuel into motive power.

INTERNAL OR EXTERNAL?
Steam engines are external combustion engines – the fuel is burned in a separate boiler (external from the engine) to make the steam that provides the motive force. Internal combustion engines, such as petrol or diesel engines, burn their fuel inside the engine.

THE FOUR STROKE ENGINE
In 1876, a German engineer Nikolaus Otto built the first four-stroke internal combustion engine. It burned a mixture of air and coal gas. Four-stroke engines get their name because the piston goes through a repetitive cycle of four up and down movements or strokes. Otto engines become widely used in European factories.

THE PETROL ENGINE
In Germany, in 1885, Gottlieb Daimler invented the petrol engine when he developed a carburettor – a device that allows a four-stroke engine to burn a mixture of air and petrol. The advantage of petrol is that it is much easier to store than coal gas.

THE DIESEL ENGINE
In 1893, German engineer Rudolf Diesel invented a four-stroke engine that burned a mixture of air and diesel oil.

A Nikolaus Otto four-stroke engine.

HENRY FORD 1863 – 1947

Nationality: American

Profession: Engineer and businessman

Biographical information: Henry Ford left school at 15 and apprenticed as a machinist. Later he set up a sawmill and engineering workshop on his father's farm. He built his first car in a workshop behind his home in Detroit in 1896. In 1903, he set up the Ford Motor Company.

Most famous invention: In 1913, Ford invented an efficient way of making cars – the assembly line. The car moves along a track in the factory, and each worker adds one part to the car as it passes them.

Eureka moment: Ford realised that if he could produce cars cheaply enough, he could sell them in huge numbers and make big profits!

Henry Ford.

FIRST OIL WELL

- In 1859, Edwin Drake drilled the world's first oil well in Pennsylvania, USA. He struck oil 21 m below the surface.

Edwin Drake (right) in 1866 in front of the first US oil well.

- At first, oil refineries concentrated on producing lubricating oils and paraffin for lamps, but after 1900, with the development of the internal combustion engine, petrol and diesel fuel quickly became the most important refinery products.

SUPER STEAM

THE MALLARD

The fastest ever steam locomotive was the Mallard. It achieved a maximum speed of 202 km/h in England in 1938. It was built by the British engineer Sir Nigel Gresley.

TIMELINE: STEAM POWER

Cugnot's steam-powered tricycle had a top speed of 3 km/h.

At first steam power was mostly used to run stationary machines. It was only through the vision and determination of engineers and inventors that steam was eventually used to power the railways.

1698 - THE STEAM PUMP
In England, engineer Thomas Savery invents a pump that uses condensed steam to create a vacuum which draws water up a pipe. The machine is used to pump water from underground mines.

1712 - THE BEAM ENGINE
English engineer Thomas Newcomen invents the first true steam engine. It uses a pair of pistons in cylinders to tilt the ends of a centrally positioned horizontal beam which operates a pump.

1769 - A STEAM WAGON
French army engineer Nicholas Cugnot builds the world's first steam-powered land vehicle. Cugnot's prototype three-wheeled artillery tractor can pull loads of up to 3 tonnes. However, the weight of the huge copper boiler at the front makes it difficult to steer. On its first trip, it runs into a wall!

1791 - ROTARY POWER
Scottish engineer James Watt perfects a steam engine which is capable of powering other machines. Watt's machine has a flywheel, which converts the up and down movement of a piston into rotary motion.

1801-1808 - RAILWAY LOCOMOTIVES
Richard Trevithick builds a steam locomotive for an ironworks in Coalbrookdale, in Shropshire, England. In 1808, he gives rides to passengers around a circular track built in London in his 'Catch me who can' steam train.

1807 - STEAMBOAT SERVICE
In the USA, the engineer Robert Fulton starts a steamboat service on the Hudson River between the cities of New York and Albany. The service is reliable and successful.

1830 - THE ROCKET
A 64-kilometre railway line between the English cities of Liverpool and Manchester is built primarily to carry passengers. A locomotive named 'Rocket', designed by the engineer Robert Stephenson, pulls the first train in 1830. For a short stretch Rocket reaches 58 km/h.

Stephenson's Rocket locomotive sits next to a larger, more modern British steam locomotive.

FASTEST ON FOUR WHEELS

1899 – 100 km/h barrier
The French engineer Camille Jenatzy builds an electric car that becomes the first vehicle to break the 100 km/h barrier.

1906 – Stanley steamer
A 'Stanley Steamer' built by the American brothers Francis and Freelan Stanley reaches a road speed of 205 km/h.

1921 – 335 km/h
French driver Sadi Lecointe reaches 335 km/h in a petrol-engine Nieuport-Delage racing car.

1988 – Solar power
In the USA, driver Molly Brennan achieves a top speed of 78 km/h in a solar-powered vehicle called Sunraycer.

1997 – Sound barrier
In the Black Rock Desert, Nevada, Andy Green breaks the sound barrier in Thrust SSC reaching a speed of 1,228 km/h.

ON THE ROAD TIMELINE

1952 – Airbag
First patented in 1952, by American John W. Hetrick, and with a practical version developed in 1973, airbags were fitted to most cars in the USA by 1988, and later to European cars.

1959 – Seat belt
First fitted to a 1959 Volvo, Nils Bohlin's 'lap-and-diagonal' design seat belts anchor passengers to the car. Seat belts have since prevented millions of injuries.

1954 – Breathalyzer
Chemicals which turn from orange to green, indicating the amount of alcohol in the breath, are the secret of the device invented by US policeman Robert Borkenstein.

- See page 52 INVENTORS AT WORK for more travel-related inventions.

PLANES & BOATS

1485 – Flapping design
The Italian artist and inventor Leonardo da Vinci sketches a man-powered aircraft made of wood and fabric. Da Vinci's design is intended to imitate the flight of birds with flapping wings.

1804 – Fixed wings
In England, the amateur flight enthusiast and inventor George Caley builds a model fixed-wing glider that establishes the basic configuration of the modern aircraft. The glider was strong enough to carry a boy, and a later, stronger model carries Caley's coachman across a narrow valley. Following the flight, the coachman hands in his notice!

1896 – Hang glider
In Germany, the inventor Otto Lilienthal is killed after crashing into the ground while testing his latest design for a hang glider. Previously Lilienthal had successfully flown distances of more than 200 metres and had made more than 2,500 flights.

1903 – Powered flight
Orville and Wilbur Wright achieve the world's first powered flight.

1907 – First helicopter
French mechanic Paul Cornu becomes the first person to build and fly a helicopter. It hovers just off the ground for 20 seconds, then the fuselage rotates in the opposite direction to the rotor blades causing the machine to crash to the ground.

1909 – Cross-channel flight
French engineer and aviator Louis Bleriot makes the first flight across the English Channel in the Type XI monoplane that he has designed and built.

1919 – First across ocean
Setting off from Newfoundland and landing in Ireland, the English pilots John Alcock and Arthur Brown fly a Vickers Vimy biplane across the Atlantic Ocean. The engines get blocked by ice several times and Brown has to clamber along the wings to chip away the ice with a knife.

• The TIMELINE continues on page 29.

Until the invention of powered flight, the only way to cross seas and oceans was by ship. Early sailors in wooden sailing ships were constantly at the mercy of the winds and high seas. In the 19th century, technological innovations, such as iron hulls and steam engines, made shipping faster, safer, and more reliable. Since the beginning of the 20th century, the development of aircraft has shrunk long-distance journey times from weeks to a matter of hours!

THE STORY OF THE FIRST FLIGHT

- 17 December, 1903, Wilbur and Orville Wright travel to sand dunes outside Kitty Hawk in North Carolina, USA, with their plane, *Flyer*.

- Only five people are witness to the world's first powered flight.

- Wilbur runs alongside Flyer holding one wing to balance the plane on the track.

- Orville operates the controls lying face down on the lower wing.

- The flight lasts 12 seconds and covers a distance of 36.5 m. The brothers make a further three successful flights that day.

ORVILLE AND WILBUR WRIGHT

Wilbur: 1867 – 1912
Orville: 1871 – 1948

Nationality: American

Profession: Engineers

Biographical information: Orville and Wilbur Wright were brothers. From an early age they were interested in engineering. They owned a business manufacturing and designing bicycles.

Most famous invention: The aeroplane – they demonstrated the first powered, controlled and sustained flight in their plane, Flyer.

Eureka moment: In 1899 Wilbur, while watching birds, realised that an aeroplane must be able to bank to one side or another, to climb or descend, and to steer to the left or right.

Inventors at work: The Wright brothers built gliders (to perfect the controls for their plane), a lightweight petrol engine (to power it) and an efficient propeller. They even built a wind tunnel to aid their experiments. The brothers approach to inventing was scientific – they thought about a machine's requirements in advance, rather than *'building the machine and seeing what happened'* like their aviation predecessors.

The Wright brothers' plane, Flyer, at Kitty Hawk.

INVENTING THE JET ENGINE

INVENTION OF THE JET ENGINE
In 1930, Royal Air Force pilot Frank Whittle patented his idea for the jet engine – an aircraft engine that uses a jet of heated air to produce thrust.

Whittle recognised the potential for an aircraft which could fly at high speeds. He proved mathematically that his invention could work, but the British Air Ministry were not interested.

THE FIRST JET ENGINE
Whittle built his jet engine and on 12 April, 1937, the turbojet engine had its maiden run on the ground. However, it was German inventors who developed the first operational jet aircraft in 1939.

Whittle's jet engine

TEST PILOTS

Test pilots make aircraft inventions possible. They put new designs of air and spacecraft through manoeuvres designed to test the machines' capabilities.

In 1947, the sound barrier was broken for the first time by American test pilot Chuck Yeager in the air-launched, rocket-powered Bell X-1 aircraft. The X-I reached 1078 km/h at an altitude of 12,800 metres.

TIMELINE: THE BALLOON INVENTORS

1783 - FIRST HUMAN FLIGHT
The first humans to fly take to the skies in a hot-air balloon invented and built by French brothers Jacques and Joseph Montgolfier.

• See page 48
JOSEPH AND JACQUES MONTGOLFIER.

1783 - HYDROGEN BALLOON
Shortly after the Montgolfiers' hot-air balloon flight, the French scientist Jacques-Alexandre-Cesar Charles makes the first flight in a balloon containing lighter-than-air hydrogen gas. Charles's balloon travels 46.5 kilometres.

1900 - ZEPPELINS
In Germany, LZ-1 the first large airship, designed by the engineer Ferdinand von Zeppelin, successfully takes to the air. Subsequently, Zeppelins are used both for warfare, as bombers, and for carrying passengers. In 1937, the Hindenburg airship disaster brings the airship era to an abrupt end.

1932 - AUGUSTE PICCARD
Professor Auguste Piccard takes his hot-air balloon to a height of

Piccard (right) and Jones operated Breitling Orbiter 3 from this pressurised capsule which resembles a spacecraft.

17,000 m. Piccard risks bursting blood vessels and his eardrums, and even black-outs because his capsule is not pressurised as modern aircraft are today.

1961 - RECORD-BREAKER
A US Navy research helium balloon carries two pilots, Malcolm Ross and Vic Parther, to an altitude of 34,668 m above the Earth's surface.

1999 - WORLD CIRCUMNAVIGATION
Balloon enthusiasts Bertrand Piccard and Brian Jones circumnavigate the world (40,814 kilometres) in Breitling Orbiter 3. The helium balloon uses air currents to control its course. Orbiter 3 is 55 m high and can contain the contents of seven olympic-sized swimming pools!

THE FIRST SUBMARINE

The first submarine (a wooden rowing boat with a watertight cover of greased leather) was designed in 1620 by the Dutch engineer Cornelius van Drebel.

The craft was powered by 12 oarsmen and reached depths of nearly 5 m during tests on the River Thames in England. Passengers breathed through tubes that ran from the submarine to the surface of the water.

SHIP INNOVATIONS

1783
French engineers demonstrate that a steam engine can be used to propel a 150-tonne riverboat.

1786
American engineer John Fitch designs and launches the world's first purpose-built steamboat on the Delaware River near the city of Philadelphia.

1838
Swedish engineer John Ericsson uses his ship Archimedes to demonstrate that a steam-driven screw (propeller) is more efficient than a steam-driven paddlewheel.

INVENTION OF THE HOVERCRAFT

- In 1955, British engineer Christopher Cockerell patented the hovercraft, a vehicle that moves on a cushion of air.

- In 1958, his prototype SR.N1 crossed the English Channel (34 kilometres) in 20 minutes.

- Cockerell patented around 70 inventions during his lifetime.

SR.N1 arrives at Dover after the first Channel crossing.

LONGITUDE

In the 18th century sailors could tell their latitude (position north-south) by taking sightings of the Sun. Longitude (position east-west) was difficult.

Comparing the time at home (using a clock) with the time at sea, according to the position of the sun, was one way to calculate the distance travelled, but no pendulum clock could keep accurate time on rolling seas.

In 1761, clockmaker John Harrison invented a chronometer (a large watch-like clock) with a mechanism and dials. Harrison's invention kept such accurate time, even at sea, that a navigator could work out on a map where he was with an accuracy of less than a kilometre.

John Harrison's chronometer.

FLIGHT TIMELINE

1927 – Solo Trans-Atlantic
The American aviator Charles Lindberg makes the first solo flight across the Atlantic Ocean (from New York to Paris) in the Spirit of St. Louis a single-engine M62.

1930 – Jet engine
In England, Royal Air Force pilot Frank Whittle patents his idea for a jet engine.

1939 – Jet aircraft
In Germany, the He 178 monoplane, designed by Ernst Heinkel, makes its first flight powered by a jet engine developed by engineer Pabst von Ohain.

1941 – Sikorsky helicopter
Russian-born aviator, Igor Sikorsky solves the problem of 'torque' (the body of a helicopter turning in the opposite direction to the rotor blades) by fitting a small rotor on the tail. His VS300 hovers in the air for 102 minutes.

1952 – Jet Airliner
The world's first jet airliner, the de Havilland Comet, comes into service, carrying passengers between London, England, and Johannesburg in South Africa.

1970 – Jumbo jet
The first Boeing 747 jumbo jet airliner comes into service between New York and London. The jumbo jet can carry more than 360 passengers at a time.

1979 – Human-powered
American pilot Bryan Allen achieves the first human-powered cross-channel flight flying the pedal-powered Gossamer Albatross aircraft designed by aeronautical engineer Paul MacCready.

1986 – Around the world
American pilots Richard Rutan and Jeana Yeager fly non-stop around the world in the experimental Voyager aircraft. The flight, which lasts nine days, is made without refuelling.

•The TIMELINE continues on page 31.

When the American colonies declared their independence in 1776, it took 48 days for the news to cross the Atlantic. The arrival of the telegraph in 1843, and the telephone in 1876, meant that news could get to anywhere in the world almost instantly. The arrival of radio communication in 1896 meant that sounds could travel vast distances without the need for cables, and in 1936, moving pictures and sounds could be seen by millions, at the same time, with the invention of television.

Wheatstone and Cooke's five-needle telegraph.

CHAPPE'S TELEGRAPH

- In 1793, France was at war. A quick way to warn of an invasion was needed. In 1794, Claude Chappe invented the telegraph.

- Chappe's telegraph used two arms at the top of a tall tower. Ropes and pulleys moved the arms into different positions each representing a letter.

- The towers were positioned 10 to 30 kilometres apart and the messages were read by people using telescopes.

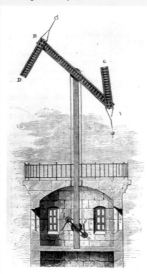

The main pole of the telegraph was about 6 metres tall.

MORSE CODE

- Samuel Morse invented Morse code in 1838. He first got the idea for the code in 1832 when he was told about experiments with electricity.

- Morse's idea was to develop a code based on interrupting the flow of electricity so that a message could be heard.

- Morse code works very simply. Electricity is either switched on or off. When it is on, it travels along a wire. At the other end of the wire the electric current can either make a sound or be printed out.

- A short electric current, a 'dit', is printed as a dot and a longer 'dah' is printed as a dash.

A	• —	N	— •
B	— • • •	O	— — —
C	— • — •	P	• — — •
D	— • •	Q	— — • —
E	•	R	• — •
F	• • — •	S	• • •
G	— — •	T	—
H	• • • •	U	• • —
I	• •	V	• • • —
J	• — — —	W	• — —
K	— • —	X	— • • —
L	• — • •	Y	— • — —
M	— —	Z	— — • •

The full Morse code is based on combining dots and dashes to represent the letters of the alphabet.

• See page 48 SAMUEL MORSE.

THE INVENTION OF THE POSTAGE STAMP

- In the early 1800s, postage in Britain was charged by distance and the number of sheets in a letter. The recipient paid for the postage not the sender.

- In 1837, retired English schoolteacher Rowland Hill wrote a pamphlet calling for cheap, standard postage rates, not charged by distance.

- The British Post Office took up Hill's ideas, and, in May 1840, issued the first adhesive, penny, postage stamps.

- The stamps were printed with black ink and become known as 'Penny Blacks'.

ALEXANDER GRAHAM BELL 1847 – 1922

Nationality: Scottish-born American
Profession: Teacher and inventor

Biographical information:
Bell left school at 14 and trained in the family business of teaching elocution. His family moved to Canada in 1870. He trained people in his father's system of teaching deaf people to speak.

Most famous invention: Working at night with his assistant, Thomas Watson, he made the first working telephone in 1876.

Inventors at work: The telegraph already used electricity to convey messages over long distances. The telephone had to turn sound into electricity and back again. To make it work was a technical challenge, which Bell and Watson solved by hard work over many months.

Eureka moment: The first words spoken down a telephone were, "Mr Watson, come here, I want you!" Bell was testing out his newly invented telephone when he spilt some chemicals on his clothes and called to his assistant for help.

Alexander Graham Bell opens the New York to Chicago telephone line in 1892.

Bell experimented for many years with different ways of sending and receiving spoken messages. This *Gallows Frame* transmitter was one of his earliest machines.

THE INVENTION OF DIRECT DIALLING

- At first, telephone connections were made by operators pushing plugs into sockets.

- In 1889, in Kansas City, USA, undertaker Almon Strowger discovered that his local operator was married to a rival undertaker and was diverting his customers' calls to her husband.

- Strowger invented the first automatic telephone switch – a remote controlled switch that could connect one phone to any of several others by electrical pulses without the need for an operator!

MOBILE PHONES AND TEXT MESSAGING

1973 – First mobile call
The first call made on a mobile phone was made in April by Dr. Martin Cooper, general manager of Motorola. He called his rival, Joel Engel, Bell Laboratories head of research.

1992 – First text
The first text message was sent. It is reported that the message was from Neil Papworth of Vodaphone and it said, "Merry Christmas".

2000 – Camera phone
The camera phone is created by

SHARP in Japan. It is called the J-Sh04.

August 2001
The first month in which over one billion text messages were sent by mobile phones.

VIDEO PHONES

- The first videotelephone with a screen for moving pictures was invented by AT&T in 1964. It allowed people to look at the people they were calling.

- Using mobile phones to record videos started with the creation of 3G mobile phones by Dr Irwin Jacobs in 2003.

TELEGRAPH & TELEPHONE TIMELINE

1861 – The pantelegraph
The first fax machine is sold. It is called the pantelegraph.

Telegraphs can be sent from one end of America to the other.

1865 – Public fax
The first fax service opens in France. It is used to send photographs to newspapers.

1866 – Atlantic cable
The ship, the 'Great Eastern', lays a second cable along the Atlantic seafloor.

1876 – Bell's telephone
Alexander Graham Bell invents the first successful telephone.

1878 – Thomas Edison
American inventor Thomas Edison has also been working on a telephone, but Bell beats him to it! Edison invents a microphone that makes the voice of the person speaking much clearer to the listener.

1880 – First pay phone
The first pay-phones open in New York.

There are now nine separate cables between America and Britain.

1892 – Direct-dial
The first direct-dial telephones become operational.

1915 – First Atlantic calls
Telephone calls across the Atlantic can be made for the first time.

1936 – Co-axial cable
The first co-axial cable is laid. This allows lots of telephone messages to pass along the same cable.

1963 – 160 Million phones
The number of telephones in the world reaches 160 million.

1988 – Fibre-optic cable
The first fibre-optic cable is laid across the Atlantic. Now telephone messages are carried on pulses of light.

- For more information on Edison:
- See page 36 EDISON'S PHONOGRAPH.
- See page 49 THOMAS ALVA EDISON.

RADIO TIMELINE

1873 - Electromagnetic waves
The Scottish scientist James Clark Maxwell prepares a paper in which he writes about electromagnetic waves that can travel through the air. He could not prove they existed.

1887 - Heinrich Hertz
The German scientist Heinrich Hertz transmits a spark using a tuned antenna. He also proves James Clark Maxwell's theory about the existence of radio waves, which are one kind of electromagnetic wave. However, the radio waves he created could not travel very far.

1894 - Marconi's bell
Marconi makes a bell ring by using radio waves to activate it.

1897 - Shore to ship
Marconi transmits a signal from land to a ship 29 kilometres out at sea. The British Royal Navy shows a great interest in this new invention.

1901 - Atlantic signal
Marconi sends a radio signal across the Atlantic Ocean.

1906 - Triode valve
The triode valve is invented by Lee DeForrest. It makes radio signals more powerful.

1906 - First voice and music
The American scientist Reginald A. Fessenden transmits his voice and broadcasts music using radio waves. Before this only Morse Code could be carried on radio waves. Following his groundbreaking achievement, Fessenden did not pursue his radio experiments.

1920 - First radio station
The world's first ever commercially licensed radio station, KDKA Philadelphia, makes its first broadcast on 2 November.

1923 - Atlantic voice
The first ever broadcast of a voice across the Atlantic Ocean from Pittsburgh, USA, to Manchester, England.

1995 - Digital radio
BBC radio stations begin digital broadcasting.

GUGLIELMO MARCONI 1874 - 1937

Marconi in 1896, with some early apparatus.

Nationality: Italian

Profession: Physicist

Biographical information: Marconi attended technical college in Italy, where he studied electricity and magnetism. After leaving college he continued his experiments at his family's farm, but could find little support for his work in Italy, so in 1896, he went to live in England.

Most famous invention: Marconi invented the first practical system of wireless communication using radio waves. In 1896, before leaving Italy, Marconi managed to transmit a radio signal over a distance of about 1.5 kilometres. In England he quickly increased the range to about 100 kilometres, and in 1899, made radio contact between Britain and France.

Eureka moment: In 1901, Marconi successfully sent a radio message across the Atlantic Ocean, from Cornwall, England, to Newfoundland, in Canada, a distance of more than 4,000 km.

Inventor at work: Marconi continued to make numerous improvements to radio transmitting and receiving equipment. In 1909, he was awarded the *Nobel Prize for Physics*.

CLOCKWORK RADIO

- In 1991, British inventor Trevor Baylis invented the wind-up radio, enabling millions in the developing world, with no permanent electricity supply, to receive broadcasts.

- The radio works by winding up a spring, which slowly uncoils and powers a small generator.

Inventor Trevor Baylis with his clockwork radio.

RADIO ON THE MOVE

Invented in 1947, the transistor replaced the valves inside radios that picked up radio signals. Transistors were much smaller than valves, so it now became possible to make portable radios.

1954
The world's *'first pocket radio'* goes on sale on 18th October. The Regency TR1 is just 12 cm high. Around 100,000 TR1s are sold during the radio's only year of production.

1955
A Japanese company called Tokyo Tsushin Kogyo decide to build a portable radio for the US market. Before they begin selling the radio, they change the company name to something Americans can easily say — the new company name is Sony.

A 1962 Sony transistor radio with a wind up watch and alarm.

JOHN LOGIE BAIRD 1888 – 1946

Nationality: Scottish

Profession: Electrical engineer

Biographical information: Baird studied at the University of Glasgow where he first became interested in the idea of using radio waves to transmit pictures. At the time, most scientists considered such a system to be impossible.

Most famous invention: Television! In 1926, using equipment that he had made himself, Baird demonstrated the world's first working television system.

Eureka moment: Baird realised that pictures could be sent by radio if the images were broken down into a series of electronic impulses. He invented a mechanical scanner that, by 1926, was able to scan and transmit moving images.

Other inventions: Baird also demonstrated colour television in 1928 and continued to work researching stereoscopic television.

In 1936, he demonstrated his mechanical system to the BBC, but they chose an electronic system from EMI.

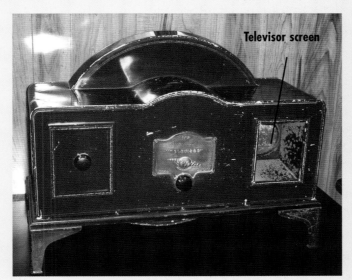

Televisor screen

The televisor, a mechanical television set devised by Baird. Viewers watched the first television broadcasts on these sets.

SATELLITES

Much of our long-distance communication relies on the hundreds of satellites that are in orbit around the Earth.

• Each satellite receives a radio or television signal from one place and then transmits it onwards.

• In summer 1962, the USA launched the 'Telstar' satellite. Telstar provided a radio and television link between Europe and America for just a few hours every day.

• Most of the satellites in orbit today are geo-stationary – they are travelling at the same speed as the Earth's rotation and will always be at the same point in the sky.

Telstar.

THE ELECTRONIC TV PIONEERS

Vladimir Zworykin, vice president of RCA (c1951).

Baird is credited with the invention of television, but the systems we use and the TVs we watch today owe much to earlier inventors (see timeline, right) and to two pioneers of electronic television, Zworykin and Shoenberg.

Vladimir Zworykin

• Russian born Vladimir Zworykin emigrated to the USA in 1919.

• Zworykin was the first to take up the suggestion by Scottish engineer Alan Campbell Swinton that it should be possible to both create and display pictures using a cathode ray tube.

• In 1931, heading a team at Radio Corporation of America (RCA), Zworykin created the first successful electronic camera tube, the iconoscope.

Isaac Shoenberg

• Russian-born Isaac Shoenberg also emigrated to Britain, in 1914.

• In 1936, working with a team at Electrical and Musical Industries (EMI), Schoenberg used Zworykin's basic idea to develop the Emitron tube.

The winning system

In 1936, EMI's electronic television system (which used the Emitron tube) was demonstrated to the BBC. It was chosen over John Logie Baird's mechanical system. Except for some detailed differences, the EMI system is still in use today.

TELEVISION TIMELINE

1860s — Pantelegraph
The Italian physicist, Abbe Giovanni Caselli, sends images over a long distance, using a system he calls the 'pantelegraph'. Caselli's system is the first prototype of a fax machine.

1873 — Pictures into signals
Two British telegraph engineers, May and Smith, find a way of turning pictures into electrical signals.

1884 — Mechanical TV
German engineer Paul Nipkow discovers television's scanning principle. His invention, a rotating disc with spirals of apertures that pass successively across the picture will make a mechanical television system possible.

1897 — Cathode-ray tube
Karl Ferdinand Braun, a German physicist, invents the first cathode-ray tube. This is used in all modern television cameras and TV sets.

1906-1907 — First TV
Boris Rosing of Russia develops a system combining the cathode ray with a Nipkow disc, creating the world's first working television system. In 1907, Rosing transmits black and white silhouettes of simple shapes.

1924 — First moving image
The Scottish engineer John Logie Baird is the first to transmit a moving image, using a system based on Nipkow's disc.

1925 — First face on TV
John Logie Baird transmits recognisable human faces.

1926 — Moving objects
Baird demonstrates the televising of moving objects at the Royal Institute.

1936 — The BBC
The BBC starts the world's first public television service in London.

1951 — Colour TV
The first colour television transmissions begin in the USA.

1989 — Satellite TV
The first satellite television stations are launched with four channels available from Sky.

1998 — Digital TV
The first digital satellite television stations are launched.

HOME INVENTIONS TIMELINE

1740 – Franklin stove
American Benjamin Franklin invents a simple, cast-iron stove (similar to modern-day woodburners) for warming homes.

1792 – Gas lighting
In 1792, Scottish engineer William Murdock invents gas lighting. He heats coal in a closed vessel and then pumps the gas to lights around his cottage in Cornwall, England.

1830 – Lawnmower
Patented in 1830, Edwin Budding's cylinder lawnmower makes maintaining a lawn possible for everyone. Before this, only people with a gardener or flock of sheep could maintain a lawn!

1844 - Refrigerator
American doctor John Gorrie builds a machine that uses compressed air to provide cooling air for feverish patients in his hospital. In 1851, he receives the first US patent for mechanical refrigeration.

c1860 – Linoleum
British rubber manufacturer Frederick Walton invents linoleum, a washable floor covering made from cloth covered with a linseed oil and pine resin substance.

1907 – Washing machine
US inventor Alva Fisher invents the first electric washing machine. The machine has a drum that tumbles the clothes and water backwards and forwards. The machine is called the 'Thor'.

1919 – Pop-up toaster
US inventor Charles Strite invents the first toaster to automatically stop toasting and pop out the toast when it is ready. However, it will be nine years before Otto Rohwedder invents sliced bread!

1946 – Microwave oven
In 1945, US engineer, Percy LeBaron Spencer invents the microwave oven. While working on radar, Spencer made the discovery that powerful microwaves had melted some sweets in his pocket!

• See page 44 DOMESTIC ROBOTS.

While most home and fashion-related inventions could not claim to have changed our world, they have certainly made it more colourful, comfortable and clean. Today we wear clothes and shoes made from a variety of different materials; we take it for granted that electric lights will illuminate our homes; that chilled food and drinks are in the refrigerator; and that, when we need 'to go', the toilet will flush and there will be a roll of toilet paper to hand!

THE INVENTION OF THE 'DYSON'

- In 1978, British inventor James Dyson noticed that the dust bag in conventional vacuum cleaners quickly clogged up.

- Dyson had the idea of making a bagless cleaner. It used centrifugal force to suck dust into a plastic cylinder.

- Five years and 5,127 prototypes later, Dyson was finally making and selling the *Dyson Dual Cyclone* vacuum cleaner – the first real vacuuming breakthrough since the vacuum cleaner's invention in 1901.

The Dyson DC15

• See page 56 VACUUM CLEANER.

TOILET INVENTIONS

FIRST FLUSHING TOILET
- Sir John Harington was a British poet and wit. He was a courtier to his godmother, Queen Elizabeth I.

- In 1596, he published a humorous work entitled *The Metamorphosis of Ajax* (a play on the word *jakes*, slang for lavatory). It included diagrams of a flushing toilet, or water closet (WC).

- Harington's toilet design had a bowl, a seat and a cistern of water for washing away the toilet's contents.

- Harington built just two of his toilets – one for himself and one for the queen at Richmond Palace.

THOMAS CRAPPER
- In the 1800s, toilet pioneers, such as Thomas Crapper began to develop the toilet further and produce the items we recognise today.

- Crapper registered a number of patents, including a spring-loaded loo seat which leapt up as soon as the user stood, pulling rods which automatically flushed the pan.

TOILET PAPER
- American Joseph Gayetty is credited with inventing toilet paper in 1857. Before Gayetty's invention, people tore pages out of mail order catalogues.

- In 1880, the British Perforated Paper Company invented a type of toilet paper. The shiny paper came in small sheets in a box.

THE LIGHT BULB

- Working independently, British inventor Sir Joseph Wilson Swan and American Thomas Edison each invented a light bulb.

- Swan is best known for his incandescent-filament electric lamp of 1879. It gave off light as an electric current passed through its carbon filament contained in a glass bulb.

- In America, Edison had the same idea. By 1880, he and Swan had developed efficient, long-lasting, light bulbs. In 1883, they formed the *Edison & Swan Electric Light Company*.

THE INVENTION OF JEANS

The story of the invention of the trousers that we now know as 'jeans' is basically the story of *Levi's 501 Jeans*.

- Levi Strauss ran a dry goods business in San Francisco. Strauss supplied cloth to Jacob Davis, a local tailor.

- To cure the problem of his customers ripping their work trousers, Davis came up with the idea of using metal rivets to strengthen the points of strain. This was a great success.

- Needing money to patent his invention, Davis teamed up with Strauss. On 20 May, 1873, the two men received patent no.139,121 from the US Patent Office and blue jeans were born.

- Around 1890, the 'waist overalls' as they were called were assigned the number 501.

- The name 'jeans' was coined in around 1960.

Vintage Levi 501s

THE INVENTION OF TRAINERS

The adidas Hyperride

Adolf (Adi) Dassler made his first shoes in 1920. He was just 20 years old. Dassler's vision was to provide every athlete with the best footwear for his or her discipline.

- Athletes wore special shoes from Dassler's workshop for the first time at the 1928 Olympic Games held in Amsterdam.

- By the mid 1930s, Dassler was making 30 different shoes for 11 different sports, and his company was the world's leading sports shoe manufacturer.

- In 1948, Dassler introduced *adidas* (a combination of his names) as the company name, and a year later he registered the unmistakable 'Three Stripes'.

- In 1954, when Germany won the Football World Cup, the team were wearing boots — by adidas!

Adi Dassler in his sports shoes factory.

BABY FASHION

US engineer Vic Mills, did not like the cloth nappies worn by his grandaughter, so he challenged the US company Proctor and Gamble to find a solution to the problem.

In 1961, after years of testing, Pampers (disposable nappies) were launched — an important invention for babies everywhere!

A truly practical invention.

THE INVENTION OF NYLON

While a professor at Harvard University in 1928, Wallace Carothers was hired by the chemical company DuPont. Carothers' mission was to, "Get rid of the worms!"

1928 - A SILK SUBSTITUTE
Dupont wanted Carothers to make a substitute for silk, the fine and very costly fibre which is spun by silkworms.

Carothers set to work with a team of eight people including a scientist called Julian Hill.

1930 - INVENTING PLASTICS
The teams first breakthrough was neoprene, and then soon after, a plastic nicknamed 3-16 polymer.

When Hill dipped a rod into 3-16, he could pull out a thread. The more he stretched the thread, the stronger it became.

The threads were springy as silk, could be made from oil, water and air and no silkworms were required!

1934 - NYLON
The 3-16 polymer was not suitable for cloth production as ironing melted it, but by tweaking the recipe they produced the artificial silk required. Five more years of research and the newly-named 'nylon' was ready to go.

INVENTION OF THE BRA

In 1913, New York partygoer Mary Jacob sewed together a couple of handkerchiefs and some ribbon to create the first 'bra' — a garment that suited her slinky dress better than a corset.

In 1914, after changing her name to Caresse Crosby, she patented the 'brassiere'. A large corset company purchased the idea, and within 5 years women everywhere were wearing bras.

THE MACKINTOSH

In 1823, the Scottish chemist Charles Macintosh invented a method of using rubber to produce waterproof cloth.

His name (misspelled as mackintosh or shortened to 'mac') became the popular name for a raincoat.

1877 – First recording
On 6 December, the first sound recording is made by American inventor Thomas Edison on a machine called a phonograph at his Menlo Park laboratory in New Jersey, USA.

1887 – Going flat
The first recording machines use cylinders made from tinfoil or wax. In 1887, Emile Berliner invents the gramophone. It records sound as a wiggly groove on a flat metal disc.

1898 – Magnetic recording
In Denmark, Valdemar Poulsen invents a new way of recording. His telegraphone machine records sound by magnetising a steel wire.

1931 – Tape recorder
The first tape recorders are built. Instead of steel wire, they use magnetic tape. The public sees tape recorders for the first time in Berlin in 1935.

1963 – Tape cassettes
The first tape recorders use tape that has to be threaded through the machine by hand. Then in 1963, Philips produce the compact cassette. It is easier to use – you just slot it into a recorder and press the play button.

1960s – Portable music
Early tape recorders are the size of a suitcase. Then in the 1960s, small battery-powered cassette recorders allow people to carry recorded music about with them. Soon, recorders are not much bigger than the tape cassettes they play.

1982 – Compact discs
Compact discs (CDs) go on sale. Music is recorded as microscopic pits in the silver-coloured discs.

1998 – Downloading
The first MP3 player, the MPMan, lets people download music files from the World Wide Web.

2001 – The ipod
Apple launches its own MP3 player, the iPod.

• See page 49
THOMAS ALVA EDISON.

LEISURE & TOYS

In the past, leisure pursuits were limited by the amount of free time available to people, and toys were primarily simple adaptations of everyday items. Nowadays, we have far more leisure time and spending power. For the past 150 years, inventors and innovators have used their talents to entertain us and satisfy our demands, from simple toys like LEGO to the latest equipment for downloading music.

Edison's phonograph the first sound recording machine.

MUSICAL INVENTIONS

c1700 – Clarinet
The German musician and instrument maker Johann Denner develops the clarinet from an earlier musical instrument called the chalumeau.

1709 – Piano
Italian harpsichord builder Bartolomeo Cristofori invents a touch-sensitive harpsichord. This new instrument will eventually become the piano. Harpsichords plucked their strings, but Cristofori's new instrument hits the strings with hammers, so the harder the keyboard was struck, the louder it played.

1948 – Long-playing record
Engineer Peter Goldmark develops a bendy vinyl disc for Columbia Records that can play 25 minutes of sound each side.

1949 – 45rpm single
RCA Victor brings out the 'single' – a 7-inch record which holds one song on each side.

EDISON'S PHONOGRAPH

- Shouting into the horn of Edison's phonograph (see above) made a needle vibrate and scratch a groove into tin-foil wrapped around a spinning cylinder.

- When the needle was moved back to the beginning of the cylinder, the groove made the needle vibrate.

- The tiny vibrations were made loud enough to hear by the machine's horn recreating the original sound.

THE WALKMAN

- In 1979, Sony engineers took just four days to create a prototype pocket-sized tape player with earphones, an idea devised by Masura Ibuka, the head of Sony.

- Ibuka wanted something businessmen could use to relieve the boredom of long plane journeys without disturbing other passengers.

- In June 1979, the 'Walkman' was launched.

DIGITAL MUSIC

This Diamond Rio is typical of the first generation of MP3 players.

- Old recording machines made a copy of music on a tape or disc. If the recording wasn't perfect, crackles and hisses could be heard.

- Digital recording is different. The music is changed into a number code, and it is the code that is recorded.

- A CD player or MP3 player reads the code and uses it to create the music. Crackles and hisses that are not part of the code are ignored, so the music is perfect.

TOYS AND GAMES

SCRABBLE
When he lost his job as an architect during the Great Depression in 1931, Alfred Mosher Butts invented the game Scrabble. Butts calculated the letter frequency and points value for each letter by counting the frequency of letters on the front page of the New York Times.

MONOPOLY
Monopoly was invented by American Charles B. Darrow. He sold his idea to Parker Brothers in 1935. Monopoly was a similar concept to Lizzie G. Magie's the Landlord's Game (patented 1904). Magie's game was devised as a way to highlight the potential exploitation of tenants by greedy landlords!

ROLLERSKATE
In January 1863, James Leonard Plimpton patented a four-wheeled roller skate that was capable of turning. Plimpton built a rollerskating floor in the office of his New York City furniture business.

LEGO
In 1955, under the leadership of Godfred Kirk Christiansen Lego launched the LEGO system of play which included LEGO automatic binding bricks. Christiansen's father Ole Kirk started the toy-making business in 1932. Approximately seven lego sets are sold each second!

KALEIDOSCOPE
The kaleidoscope was patented by Scottish physicist Sir David Brewster in 1817. Kaleidoscopes use mirrors to reflect images of pieces of coloured glass in geometric designs. The design can be endlessly changed by rotating the end of the kaleidoscope.

BARBIE
Barbara Millicent Roberts, or Barbie as she is better known, was launched in 1959 by California toy company Mattel Inc. Ruth Handler, co-founder of Mattel, spearheaded the doll's introduction. Mattel calculates that every second, two Barbies are sold somewhere in the world.

INVENTION OF BASKETBALL

Basketball was invented in December, 1891, by James Naismith a PE instructor at the International YMCA Training School, Springfield, Massachusetts. Basketball gets its name from the two bushel baskets (used for collecting peaches) that Naismith used as the goals.

INVENTING MOVIE SPECIAL EFFECTS

- A new type of camera, called a motion control camera, was invented by George Lucas to make the first *Star Wars* movie in 1977.

- A motion control camera is a camera moved by a computer. The computer is programmed with the camera's movements, so the camera can go through exactly the same movements again and again.

- The camera films models of spacecraft and planets, one by one. Then all the separate images are combined to form one scene.

AT THE MOVIES TIMELINE

1882 – Camera gun
Frenchman Étienne-Jules Marey is the first person to take a series of photographs quickly with one camera. The gun-like camera takes 12 photographs on a paper disc in one second. It was the fore-runner of the movie camera.

1887 – Paper to film
An American minister, Hannibal Goodwin, uses a strip of flexible film instead of light-sensitive paper to record images. Film quickly replaces paper.

1888 – First film
The first film is shot in Leeds, England, by Frenchman Louis Aimé Augustin Le Prince. It shows traffic crossing a bridge.

1891 – Kinetoscope
The American inventor Thomas Edison invents a machine called a Kinetoscope for showing films. Only one person can see the film at a time!

1895 – Cinema is born
The French brothers, Auguste and Louis Lumière, show films to the public for the first time. Cinemas quickly spread throughout France and all over the world.

1927 – Talkies
Warner Brothers make the first feature film with sound. It was called 'The Jazz Singer'. Sound movies were called 'talkies'.

1993 – Computer characters
'Jurassic Park' featured the most realistic computer-generated images (cgi) ever seen in a movie. Cgi was used to create life-like dinosaurs, which were blended with live action.

1995 – Computer movies
Disney and Pixar made the first totally computer-generated movie, 'Toy Story'.

2001 – Digital movies
The first movie shot entirely using digital cameras is 'Star Wars: Attack of the Clones'.

S ince our early ancestors wondered what would happen if they put meat on a fire, humans have enjoyed inventing with food and drink. We seek out new foods, we create new tastes and we devise new ways to grow, prepare and store our food. Today, because we know that too much fat and sugar is bad for us, scientists are hard at work making our favourite foods and treats more healthy!

GROWING FOOD TIMELINE

1492 – New foods
Columbus discovers America. In the next two hundred years, potatoes, maize, tomatoes, chillis, tobacco, and cocoa reach the rest of the world.

1701 – Seed drill
Jethro Tull invents the seed drill in England. The drill sows seed in straight lines.

1701 – Fertiliser
The first guano (seabird manure) is brought to Europe from South America to use as fertiliser.

1834 — Reaping machine
American Cyrus McCormick invents the horse-drawn reaping machine which replaces men using sickles and scythes to cut corn and make hay.

1837 – Steel plough
American John Deere invents the steel plough which can plough the soil of the American mid-west without clogging. This makes it possible for people to settle and farm in this region.

1854 - Threshing machine
An improved American threshing machine is made which can thresh 740 litres of wheat in half an hour – six men can thresh only 60 litres.

1860 - Milking machine
Modern improvements to the milking machine allow a farmer to milk six cows at once, and milk an entire herd without help.

1873 – Barbed wire
American Joseph Glidden perfects barbed wire. This invention makes fencing much cheaper for farmers.

1917 – Ford tractor
The first mass-produced tractor made by Ford goes on sale.

• See page 17
THE STORY OF GENETIC ENGINEERING.

INVENTING THE SANDWICH

- Everyone's favourite lunch was invented in the 18th century by Englishman John Montagu, the 4th Earl of Sandwich.

- The story goes that on one occasion in 1762, Montagu played cards for 24 hours non-stop. He ate beef between slices of toast so that one of his hands was free for playing cards at all times. Montagu's convenient snack was named the *sandwich* after the inventive Earl.

INVENTING COCA-COLA

- Described as the world's 'best known taste', the drink we now know as *Coca-Cola* was invented by pharmacist Dr John Stith Pemberton, in Atlanta, Georgia, USA.

- On 8 May, 1886, a jug of Dr. Pemberton's syrup was sampled at Jacobs' Pharmacy and pronounced, *"Excellent"* by the lucky customers who were gathered there. Carbonated water was added to the syrup to produce a drink that was both *"delicious and refreshing"*. The new product was immediately put on sale for 5 cents a glass.

- The inventor's partner Frank M Robertson suggested the name Coca-Cola and correctly thought that, *"the two Cs would look well in advertising"*.

The famous Coca-Cola trademark was penned in Robertson's unique script.

LOUIS PASTEUR 1822 – 1895

Nationality: French
Profession: Scientist

Biographical information: The young Louis Pasteur did not impress as a student, but classes given by a brilliant chemistry teacher were to change his life. After studying at the famous Ecole Normale Superieure in Paris, he became the Dean of the Faculty of Science at the University of Lille.

Most famous discovery: Pasteur showed that invisible organisms can spoil food and cause disease. Pasteurisation, the process he invented of making liquids hot enough to kill any harmful organisms without destroying their food value, is still used today, particularly in milk production. It is used to kill bacteria which can cause tuberculosis in humans.

Eureka moment: While studying the fermentation process of wine and vinegar he made his greatest discovery: that fermentation and decay are caused by microscopic living organisms. By heating wine to about 60ºC he killed off the unwanted yeast cells that caused the product to spoil.

Other discoveries: Vaccinations,

including a vaccine for the killer disease rabies developed from the brain tissue of infected animals. Pasteur was hailed as a hero when he cured a boy who had been bitten by a rabid dog.

• See page 23 EDWARD JENNER (for vaccinations).

CLARENCE BIRDSEYE 1886 – 1956

Nationality: American

Profession: Naturalist

Biographical information:
Clarence Birdseye was born in New York, in 1886. He studied biology at college, but left to work as a field naturalist with the US government in the frozen north of Canada.

Eureka moment: In Labrador in 1912, Birdseye watched native Americans fishing through holes chipped in an icy lake. As fish were pulled out, they were immediately frozen by the intense cold air. Birdseye realised that speedy chilling solved the main problem with frozen food which is ice!

Most famous invention: When food is frozen slowly, long, sharp crystals of ice are formed which cut into the food causing it to break up when de-frosted. It took Birdseye eight years to work out how to chill food quickly enough to stop the daggers of ice forming. By 1930, Birdseye's machine, which squeezed pre-packed food between two very cold plates, was ready to go into

Clarence Birdseye (in the white lab coat) experiments with a huge dehydration machine.

production. However, home freezers were still very rare.

It would be 1955, following the launch of the fishfinger, before Birdseye's invention of frozen food was finally a worldwide success.

THE INVENTION OF CRISPS

- In the Saratoga Springs resort, New York, USA, in 1853, customer Cornelius Vanderbilt complained that his french fries were too thick.

- The resort's chef George Crum fried up a serving of paper-thin, crunchy, crisp potatoes for Vanderbilt.

- Dubbed *'Saratoga Chips'* this new way of cooking potatoes quickly became popular.

- George Crum had invented the crisp!

INVENTING CORNFLAKES

- American Will Kellogg worked at his family's health resort which was keen to promote healthy vegetarian food.

- In 1894, while experimenting with boiled wheat, he discovered that when crushed between rollers, wheat that had been previously soaked for a long time broke up into flakes.

- *'Toasted Corn Flakes'* were sold first by mail order and then through shops. In 1906, Will parted company with his brother John who objected to the addition of sugar and salt to the cereal.

- 20 years later, Will Kellogg was a cornflake tycoon and one of the richest men in America.

CHOCOLATE CHIPS BY ACCIDENT!

- One day while preparing a batch of Butter Drop Do cookies, American Ruth Wakefield substituted a semi-sweet Nestle chocolate bar, cut up into bits, for the usual cooking chocolate she used in her cookie recipe.

- Unlike the cooking chocolate, the pieces of Nestle chocolate did not melt when they were baked, they only softened — the chocolate chip cookie was born!

CHOCOLATE DISCOVERY & INVENTION
TIMELINE

c 1000 BC
Chocolate is produced from cocoa beans. It is believed that the Olmec Indians of Central America were the first to grow cocoa beans as a crop.

Early 1500s
Christopher Columbus and later the Spanish explorer Hernando Cortes record seeing cocoa being used and bought and sold during their explorations in the Americas.

1544
Mayan nobles bring gifts of ready-to-drink, beaten chocolate to Prince Philip of Spain. It will be 100 years before Spain and Portugal export the drink to the rest of Europe.

The Spanish add cane sugar and vanilla to their cocoa drink, and coca becomes popular as a medicine.

Late 1600s
Eating solid chocolate is introduced in Europe in the form of rolls and cakes, served in chocolate emporiums.

1753
Swedish naturalist Carolus Linnaeus, dissatisfied with the word 'cocoa' renames it 'theobroma' – Greek for 'food of the gods'.

1765
Irish chocolate-maker John Hanan imports cocoa beans to the USA. Hanan and fellow American Dr. James Baker build America's first chocolate mill making 'Baker's chocolate'.

1828
Conrad Van Houten invents the cocoa press.

1847
Joseph Fry and Son create a paste that can be molded to produce the first modern chocolate bar.

1876
Milk chocolate is invented by Daniel Peter of Vevey, Switzerland after eight years of experimenting!

• The TIMELINE continues on page 41.

THE COMPUTER

Computers are now used in nearly every part of our lives, and yet the computer has only been around for just a few years. One hundred years ago, mechanical machines that did calculations were used, but it was only at the end of the 1930s that electronic computers appeared. The first computers were large machines designed for use in laboratories, in industry and for defence. In 1974, it became possible to have a computer in your home.

The Apple Macintosh, or Mac, was the first computer to have what is known as a desktop-type screen with icons.

ANCIENT COMPUTER

- The abacus was invented in the period 3000 – 1000 BC by the Babylonians (an ancient race of people living in the area that is modern-day Iraq).

- This early counting machine made up of beads on rods can be said to be the first step in the development of the computer.

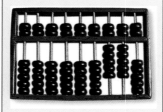

THE POTENTIAL OF AN INVENTION

As with all the greatest inventions, at first, not everyone could see the computer's potential.

"I think there is a world market for maybe five computers."
Thomas Watson, Chairman of IBM, 1943.

"There is no reason anyone in the right state of mind will want a computer in their home."
Ken Olson, President of Digital Equipment Corp, 1977.

THE FIRST COMPUTERS

ENIAC

1946 – ENIAC (Electronic Numerical Integrator and Computer) The first electronic and programmable computer. ENIAC contained over 17,000 vacuum tubes and occupied a room 15 m by 9 m!

1951 – UNIVAC 1
The world's first electronic computer to go on sale. It was created by John Eckert and John Mauchly. It was used by the US government to help gather material for the national census.

UNIVAC

APPLE II

1977 – Apple II
The first successful personal computer to go on sale. It was made by Apple Computer Inc. It was the first computer to have a colour screen and its own keyboard.

1983 – Apple Lisa
The first computer to use a mouse and pull-down menus goes on sale. Apple Lisa was also created by Apple Computer Inc.

KEY COMPUTER DEVELOPMENTS

A factory worker makes vacuum tubes.

VACUUM TUBES
The main electronic parts of early computers were called vacuum tubes, or simply valves, because they controlled the flow of electricity.

Transistors are made of materials called semiconductors.

1947 - TRANSISTORS
The first prototype transistor was invented at the Bell laboratories in the USA. The transistor acts as an electronic switch, and once it was perfected in the 1950s, it quickly replaced the vacuum tube.

This microchip, held in the jaws of an ant, contains thousands of components.

1960s - MICROCHIPS
In the late 1960s, the integrated circuit was developed. Thousands of transistors and other electric components could be built onto a tiny silicon chip, or microchip.

1968 - MICROPROCESSORS
In 1968, Ted Hoff of Intel was asked to come up with a design for a new calculator chip that could do several jobs at once. He came up with the idea of the microprocessor. Launched in 1971, the microprocessor made it possible to build much smaller computers.

INVENTIONS FOR THE COMPUTER

1964 — Inkjet printer
The first inkjet printer was invented in 1964. It was considered pretty amazing, but computer owners today would be very disappointed with the results!

1965 — The computer mouse
US engineer Doug Engelbart and his team at the Human Factors Research Center of the Stanford Research Institute, design and develop the computer mouse.

1976 — Laser printer
First laser printer introduced.

1991 — Digital camera
Kodak produces the first digital camera, the DCS100. The photos have to be stored in a separate piece of equipment.

Today's digital cameras collect 4,100,000 separate pieces of information every time you take a picture.

Computer mouse

COMPUTERS ALL AROUND

Today, the computer is in almost every electrical item we use.

MOBILE PHONE
The computer in a mobile phone works out where you are and which is the closest transmitter.

CAR
An in-car computer works out the most economical use of petrol in most modern cars.

VIDEO CAMERA
All modern video cameras include an 'auto focus' function that examines what it can see, detects the edges of each item coming through the lens, and adjusts the focus to keep pictures sharp.

AIRLINER
There are probably more computers in an airliner than any other vehicle. Computers control everything from the speed and height at which the plane flies, to the running of the in-flight movie and the cooking of your meal.

ALAN TURING 1912 – 1954

Nationality: British

Profession: Mathematician and computer expert

Biographical information: Turing was born in 1912. He had a gift for mathematics and studied this subject at Cambridge University.

Most famous invention:
Turing's work as a mathematician was stopped by World War II. He was taken to Bletchley Park, in England, where he led a team trying to find a way to crack the *Enigma code* used by Germany, Italy and Japan. In 1943, Turing designed a computer called the *Colossus* which helped to decipher the German codes, and helped win the second world war.

Eureka moment: In 1924, university student Alan Turing wrote an essay in which he described a machine that is the basis of all computers in the world today. It was the first idea for a computer to include memory, a processor and a way of storing information on tape.

Other inventions: After World War II, Turing continued working on computers. In 1950, he wrote an article in which he said that a computer could have the same intelligence as any person. Alan Turing died in 1954 after drinking poison.

COMPUTERS TIMELINE

1959 — First minicomputer
Digital Equipment Corporation produce an early minicomputer the PDP-1. It sells for $120,000 – a fraction of the cost of mainframe computers. The later model PDP-8, in 1965, uses the recently invented integrated circuit and sells for $20,000.

1967 — Computer keyboard
Keyboards are used for data entry.

1968 — Intel
Intel is formed. The company will grow to become one of the world's largest and most important computer processor manufacturers.

1970 — Floppy disk
Floppy disk is produced by IBM.

1971 — Microprocessor
First microprocessor is produced.

1974 — Personal computer
The first personal computer the Altair 8800 goes on sale. It is sold as a kit so the customer has to put the computer together before they use it.

1975 — Microsoft
Bill Gates and Paul Allen form Microsoft and adapt BASIC language for use on the Altair PC.

1976 — Apple Computer Inc
Apple Computer Inc is founded by Steve Wozniak and Steve Johns.

1981 — IBM PC
IBM launches their Personal Computer (IBM PC) which uses Microsoft Disc Operating System (MS-DOS).

1982 — The CD
Philips Electronics and Sony Corporation work together to invent the CD.

1984 — The Mac
Apple launches the Macintosh Computer, designed to appeal to those who are not computer experts.

1985 — Windows
Microsoft releases the first version of the Windows operating system.

1995 — Windows 95
Microsoft releases Windows 95 which for the first time fully integrates MS-DOS with Windows.

INTERNET TIMELINE

1960s to 1980s – ARPAnet

A team at the US Advanced Research Projects Agency (ARPA) develop a communications network between researchers and scientists in the USA.

Other organisations will join the network throughout the 1970s and early 1980s, and the network will grow and grow.

1971 – The first email

The first email is sent by computer engineer Ray Tomlinson.

1973 TO 1974 – Inventing the Internet

Vint Cerf and Bob Kahn design the Internet – a network of computers and cables. They also define the IP (Internet Protocol), the way in which information will be sent on the Internet.

1979 – Emoticons

Adding emotions to email messages is suggested, such as –) to show something is 'tongue in cheek'. By the early 1980s 'emoticons' such as :-) and :-(are in widespread use.

1980 – First virus

The first virus is accidentally released onto ARPAnet bringing the whole network to a halt.

1983 – The Internet

The Internet is launched and made available to everyone.

The Domain Name System (DNS) which takes you where you need to be on the Internet, using a web address, is invented by Paul Mockapetris.

Computer expert Fred Cohen invents the term 'computer virus'.

1987 – MP3 files

The development of the MP3 file format begins at the Fraunhofer Institut in Germany. It allows music and speech recordings to be compressed and will be used by many people on the Internet to easily copy and swap their music collections.

• The TIMELINE continues on page 43.

INTERNET & GAMES

The Internet is a worldwide collection of computers connected by cables, telephone lines and satellites. Anyone can be part of the Internet by connecting their computer to a telephone line. It allows people to send messages (emails) to anyone else who is connected, interact with other computer users wherever they are in the world and to look at information created by both large organisations and private individuals, via the World Wide Web.

TIM BERNERS-LEE

TIM BERNERS-LEE

Nationality: English

Profession: Computer scientist

Biographical information: Berners-Lee was born in London, England, in 1955. Interested in computers, he went to Oxford University. While at Oxford, he built his own computer from old electronic parts and bits of a TV. Both of his parents worked in the computer industry.

Eureka moment: Berners-Lee developed a programme called *Enquire* to help him access varied pieces of information needed in his work. The information was stored in files that contained connections, hypertext links.

Most famous invention: The World Wide Web. In 1989, while working at CERN (European Centre for Nuclear Research) in Geneva, Switzerland, Berners-Lee wrote a programme which allowed CERN's scientists to share their work through a global hypertext document system. The Web was released to the world via the Internet in 1991.

Other inventions: In 1994, Berners-Lee founded the World Wide Web Consortium. The consortium's goal is to lead the Web to its full potential in the future.

INVENTING THE INTERNET

• Internet pioneers Vint Cerf and Bob Kahn invented the Internet Protocol: the way of sending little 'packets' of information through the Internet network.

• A 'packet' is a bit like a postcard containing information.

• If the postcard has the right address, it can be given to any computer connected to the Internet, and the computer can figure out which cable to send the postcard (the 'packet') down so that it gets to the right recipient.

INVENTION OF EMAIL

In 1971, US computer scientist Ray Tomlinson devised a computer programme for sending messages on the ARPAnet network. The programme would become email, one of the main ways of communicating on the Internet.

• The first test message was sent between two machines that were physically next to each other, but only connected by ARPAnet. The test was successful — email had been invented!

• Today, Tomlinson cannot remember what the first email said, but he jokes it was probably just something like, "QWERTYUIOP".

• Probably the first email message sent to another person on ARPAnet was one announcing the new service and telling people to use @, the symbol Tomlinson chose to separate user names from host computer names.

MOSAIC

- In 1993, the world's first user-friendly web browser was developed by American Mark Andreessen and a team at the US National Center for Supercomputing Applications (NCSA).

- Mosaic used a point-and-click application which made it easy for people to navigate the World Wide Web.

- By 1994, Mosaic had several million users.

PONG

- In 1972, the Atari Corporation was founded by US computer engineers Nolan Bushnell, Ted Dabney and Al Alcorn.

- In 1972, Bushnell and team invented the video game *Pong*, based on ping-pong (table tennis).

- Two on-screen paddles knocked a ball back and forth across the screen.

- Pong became hugely popular as an arcade-style coin-operated game, and went on to be produced in a home version.

1970s poster advertising the revolutionary new game, Pong.

TIMELINE: INVENTION OF COMPUTER GAMES

1889 — NINTENDO
The Nintendo company is founded in Japan. It makes playing cards.

1958 — FIRST COMPUTER GAME
William A. Higinbotham of the Brookhaven National Laboratory in New York uses an analog computer, control boxes and an oscilloscope to create 'Tennis for Two' a game to amuse visitors to the laboratory.

1962 — SPACEWAR!
A team at the Massachusetts Institute of Technology in the US, invent a game as part of a programme to demonstrate the new PDP-1 computer. The game, which would now look extremely simple, involves players moving spaceships and firing torpedoes.

1972 — PONG
The Atari Corporation invents Pong.

1977 — MISSILE ATTACK
Mattel releases the first handheld game, but it uses small lights rather than a screen to display graphics.

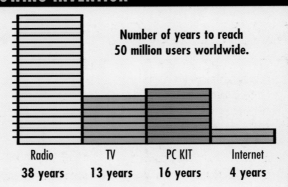

1980 — BATTLEZONE
The first 3D game is produced. 'Battlezone' is such a breakthrough that the US Government uses it to train troops.

1989 — NINTENDO GAMEBOY
Video games go handheld with the release of the first Nintendo Gameboy.

1994 — PLAYSTATION
Sony releases the PlayStation, but only in Japan. It reaches the rest of the world the following year.

2000 — PLAYSTATION 2
It is even more successful than the original PlayStation, selling out worldwide within days.

In 2000, Nintendo sells its one hundred millionth Gameboy.

2002 - X-BOX
Microsoft enters the console market as it launches the X-Box.

> • *See page 54 INVENTORS AT WORK – OSCILLOSCOPE*

See page 54 INVENTORS AT WORK – OSCILLOSCOPE

A FAST-GROWING INVENTION

In 1998, the US Department of Commerce report *The Emerging Digital Economy* stated that, *"The Internet's pace of adoption eclipses all other technologies that preceded it"*.

When radio was invented it took 38 years to reach 50 million users. The internet took just 4 years.

Number of years to reach 50 million users worldwide.

Radio	TV	PC KIT	Internet
38 years	13 years	16 years	4 years

INTERNET TIMELINE

1988 – Internet worm
Robert Morris, a US science student unleashes an Internet worm (a programme that propagates itself across a network) onto the Internet. The Morris Worm brings 6000 computers to a halt.

1989 – Inventing www
Tim Berners-Lee invents the World Wide Web – a way for computer users to access many different types of information from different sources.

1991 – WWW on the Internet
The World Wide Web is launched and made available to the world via the Internet.

1992 – Surfing
The term 'surfing the Internet' is used for the first time by American librarian and Internet expert Jean Armour Polly.

1993 – Mosaic
The first web browser is created. It is called 'Mosaic'.

1994 – Yahoo!
The Yahoo! search engine is created in April 1994 by David Filo and Jerry Yang, two PhD students at Stanford University, California. They invent the directory as a way of keeping track of their interests and finding cool websites for their friends.

1995 – Internet Explorer
Launched in July 1995 as part of the Windows 95 package, Internet Explorer 1.0 makes the Internet accessible to more people.

1995 – Online music
RealAudio is launched. This software makes it possible for Internet users to listen to live music and radio online.

1995 – Online bookshop
amazon.com is launched by US computer scientist Jeff Bezos. The company is started in Bezos's garage!

2000 – Web movie
The science-fiction movie 'Quantum Project' is the first movie made specially to be seen on the Internet instead of in a cinema.

2002 – Internet users
The number of Internet users is put at 604,111,719 worldwide.

RoboSapien

The word *robot* was first used by the Czech writer Karel Capek. It means 'forced labour', and is a good way of describing what robots are for. Robots can do many jobs that humans can do, but they can also tackle jobs that a human would find too difficult, or too dangerous. Robots are currently used in factories, they explore outer space and the inside of volcanoes, and they appear in our homes as toys or cyber (robotic) pets.

ROBOTICS TIMELINE

1495 – Da Vinci's Knight
Leonardo da Vinci builds a mechanical device that looks like a knight in armour. The mechanism inside makes it look as though the knight is moving.

1898 – Robotic boat
Nikola Tesla builds and shows a robotic boat at Madison Square Gardens, New York, USA.

1921 – A new word
The Czech writer Karel Capek introduces the word 'Robot' in his play 'RUR'.

1946 – George Devol
American inventor George Devol invents a remote-control device that can tell another machine which direction to move in.

1962 – The Ultimate
The first industrial arm robot, the Ultimate, is used at a car factory.

1966 – Shakey
Shakey the robot is built. 'Shakey' is designed to remember what it did in the past and then behave differently in the future. It moves on wheels and is connected by radio to a computer. It was built at the Stanford Research Institute in California, USA. The name tells you how well it moved!

1969 – Stanford Arm
Victor Scheinman, a student at the Stanford Artificial Intelligence Lab in California, USA, creates the 'Stanford Arm'. This design becomes the standard for robot arms.

1970 – Stanford Cart
The 'Stanford Cart' is built by Hans Moravec. Its movement is controlled remotely by computer. The Stanford cart travels on large wheels and can make its way around an obstacle course by using a camera.

1974 – The Silver Arm
Victor Scheinman starts selling the 'Silver Arm'. It can put together small parts using touch sensors. It is sold to engineering factories.

• The TIMELINE continues on page 45.

The AIBO robotic pet dog. AIBO dogs can even play football!

MOSRO – THE ROBOT SECURITY GUARD

- MOSRO patrols factories and shopping centres.
- MOSRO can detect gas, smoke and movement using a camera and infrared detectors.
- MOSRO issues warnings in over 20 languages.

This is the MOSRO MINI mobile security robot. It is just 28 cm tall.

DOMESTIC ROBOTS

ROBOMOW RL1000 (2003)
Can mow lawns without any help. It can cut grass to six different heights. It is just over 30 cm high.

CYE ROBOT (2003)
A robot butler. It can carry dishes, deliver letters and help guests find their way around a house. It can be controlled through the Internet.

MARON (2002)
Can be controlled with a mobile phone. It can detect intruders in a house, take photographs and can operate dishwashers and video recorders.

Maron

CYBER PETS

A robot dog first made an appearance at the New York World's Fair in 1939. Today, cyber pets can behave just like real animals.

AIBO DOGS
The latest cyber dogs made by Sony can play, walk, obey spoken commands and even recognise the voices and faces of their owners.

ROBOSAPIEN
This human-like cyber pet can run, disco dance, throw things, pick things up and try karate. RoboSapien can even swear and break wind!

TAKARA AQUAROID FISH
This cyber pet can be put into an aquarium. It looks like a fish, it moves away from strong light and can swim at two different speeds.

TOMY HUMAN DOG
This cyber pet (built by Tomy) can walk, sit, sing tunes and has 16 different personalities.

INVENTING HAZBOTS

Robots that do dangerous jobs which cannot be done by people are sometimes called 'Hazbots'.

RADIOACTIVITY

In 1999, a hazbot called 'Pioneer' was used at the Chernobyl nuclear power station, the site of the worst nuclear accident in history. Pioneer went into the burned-out, radioactive power station to test for levels of radioactivity and to test the structure of the remaining building. Pioneer was built by a team from the Carnegie Mellon University and Redzone Robotics.

BOMB DISPOSAL

The British army have used bomb disposal robots since the early 1970s. The first was called 'Wheelbarrow'.

NATURAL HAZARDS

Robots can be used to investigate volcanoes. A robot called Dante II explored an Alaskan volcano in 1994. Dante II can be remotely controlled or it can move by itself.

FIREFIGHTING

Robots are used in firefighting because they are not affected by the heat and smoke. Robug-3 is a fire-fighting robot designed at Portsmouth University, in the UK. It has eight legs and suckers which allow it to climb walls and move across ceilings. Robug-3 can also pull very heavy weights.

THE INVENTION OF MINI-ROBOTS

At the US Department of Energy's Sandia National Laboratories, scientists are developing the world's smallest autonomous, untethered robot.

- The mini-robot has 8 kilobytes of memory, is a centimetre high and weighs less than 30 grams.

- The mini-robot is powered by watch batteries and future enhancements could include a miniature camera, a microphone or chemical sniffers.

- The mini-robot travels on two track wheels at a speed of 50 cm per minute.

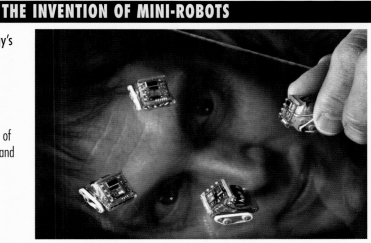

The mini-robots could travel in swarms like insects and fit into tiny spaces, such as pipes.

- Future uses could include detecting chemical or biological weapons; disabling land mines; or missions as a mini spy — taking photographs of secret papers without being seen!

ROBOTS IN SPACE

1997 — CASSINI-HUYGENS
Studying the planet Saturn, its rings and moons.

2003 — SMART 1
Searching the moon for frozen water, and for new minerals and chemicals on the moon's surface.

2003 — BEAGLE 2
Designed to investigate the surface of Mars. However, there was no contact after touchdown.

2003 — SPIRIT AND OPPORTUNITY
Studied the soil and rocks of Mars.

2004 — ROSETTA
Will meet with a comet in 2014 and investigate the comet's surface.

GEORGE DEVOL

Nationality: American

Profession: Engineer and inventor

Biographical information:
Devol was born in February 1912, in Louisville, USA.
In 1939, Devol designed and built an automatic counter at the New York World's Fair. The counter kept a record of the number of visitors.

Most famous invention:
The first industrial robot.
In 1954, Devol invented the first programmable robot. He did not use the word *robot* but *Universal Automation*. Devol founded the world's first robot building company that built robots called *Unimation* for lifting and stacking hot pieces of metal in a car factory.

Other inventions: During World War II, Devol helped to build systems that could protect aircraft from radar. They were used during the D-Day landings in Europe, in 1944.

ROBOTICS TIMELINE

1976 — Soft Gripper
The Japanese 'Soft Gripper' is invented by Shigeo Hirose of the Tokyo Institute of Technology. This robot arm can wrap itself around objects like a snake.

1977 — Voyagers
The deep space explorers Voyagers 1 and 2 are launched from the Kennedy Space Flight Center, in the USA.

1981 — Direct drive arm
The first 'direct drive arms' are built. They have motors in the joints of the arms. This makes them faster and more accurate than older robotic arms. They are designed by Takeo Kanade, Professor of Robotics at Carnegie Mellon University, in the USA.

1989 — Genghis
A walking robot called 'Genghis' is shown for the first time at the Massachusetts Institute of Technology (MIT) in the USA.

1992 — Robot wars
Combats between robots, sometimes called BattleBots, begin. The first 'Robot Wars' take place in 1994.

1994 — Dante II
A robot called 'Dante II' walks down a volcano in Alaska.

1996 — Robotuna
The first robot fish is built. It is designed by Professor Michael Triantafyllou of the Massachusetts Institute of Technology (MIT) in the USA. It is hoped that underwater robots will be able to explore parts of the ocean where humans cannot reach.

1997 — Sojourner
The robotic rover 'Sojourner' begins its exploration of the surface of the planet Mars.

1998 — The Furby
The 'Furby' goes on sale. It is the first robot toy that can respond to commands.

2000 — Asimo
The human-like robot called 'Asimo' is built by Honda. It is 1.2 m tall, walks on legs and can even walk around corners. It is designed to help around the house.

A TO Z
INVENTORS

Appert, Francois
In 1810, French chef and inventor Francois Appert invented the bottling process for storing heat-sterilised food. In 1812, he opened the world's first commercial preserved food factory, initially using glass jars and bottles. In 1822, the factory began using tin-plated metal cans.

Biro, Ladislao
The ballpoint pen was invented in the late 1930s by Hungarian brothers Ladislao and Georg Biro. Although the Biro brothers are credited with the invention of 'the biro', a similar writing instrument had been invented in 1888 by US inventor John Loud.

Celsius, Anders
In 1742, the Swedish astronomer Anders Celsius invented the Celsius (or centigrade) scale which uses 0° for the freezing point of water and 100° degrees for the boiling point.

Cousteau, Jacques
In 1943, French explorer Jacques Cousteau and engineer Emile Gagnan connected portable compressed-air cylinders, via a pressure regulator, to a mouthpiece, inventing the aqua-lung. This piece of apparatus gives divers complete freedom to explore the oceans.

Fahrenheit, Daniel
In 1714, physicist Daniel Fahrenheit invented the mercury thermometer and devised the Fahrenheit temperature scale. Fahrenheit had also invented an alcohol thermometer in 1709.

INVENTORS

An inventor is anyone who thinks of something new to make, or a new way to make or do something. We don't know the names of most of the inventors who have influenced our lives, or exactly when they made their breakthroughs. But many inventors are famous, and we even know about the *Eureka moment* when they had their brilliant idea.

ARCHIMEDES OF SYRACUSE 287 – 212 BC

The 'Archimedes Portrait' by Domenico Fetti, painted in 1620.

Nationality: Greek

Profession: Mathematician

Biographical information: Archimedes was born and worked in the city of Syracuse in Sicily, although he studied at Alexandria, in Egypt. He was killed when Roman soldiers conquered Syracuse.

Most famous invention: While wondering about how to test if a crown was made of pure gold, Archimedes discovered the *principle of buoyancy* – if an object is placed in a fluid, it will displace its own volume of fluid. This is now known as *Archimedes' principle*.

Eureka moment: Archimedes had the original 'Eureka' moment. Getting into a bath he noticed that the water rose up the sides – his body was displacing its own volume of water. He raced into the street, without any clothes, shouting, *"Eureka"* (I've found it).

• See page 52 ARCHIMEDES SCREW.

GALILEO GALILEI 1564 – 1642

Nationality: Italian

Profession: Mathematician

Biographical information: The son of a musician, Galileo went to the University of Pisa to study medicine, but eventually became a professor of mathematics. During the 1630s, Galileo was arrested and imprisoned by the Catholic Church because of his scientific views.

Most famous invention: Galileo is widely considered to be the founder of modern experimental science. He established the principle that scientific theories should be based on data (measurements) obtained from experiments.

Eureka moment: Galileo was able to devise a mathematical formula to describe the motion of falling objects. The story that he dropped identical weights of iron and feathers from the *Leaning Tower of Pisa* may not be true, but Galileo did establish that all objects fall at the same speed, no matter what their weight.

Other discoveries: Galileo was also interested in astronomy. He did not invent the telescope, but in 1609 he built his own. Galileo was able to observe the craters on our moon, he discovered Jupiter's four largest moons, and he was the first person to describe the rings of Saturn.

• See page 47 for more INFORMATION on Galileo's life and work.

Galileo on an Italian 2000 lire banknote.

LEONARDO DA VINCI 1452 – 1519

Leonardo Da Vinci

Nationality: Italian

Profession: Artist

Biographical information: Da Vinci was apprenticed to a sculptor, and worked as a painter for the rulers of Florence, Milan and France. He produced some famous paintings, including the *Mona Lisa*. Da Vinci filled thousands of pages of notebooks with drawings and notes about everything he saw around him. He studied human anatomy, military engineering, the flight of birds and the movement of water.

Most famous invention: Da Vinci's notebooks contained drawings and ideas which would not be put into practice for hundreds of years: parachutes, canals, armoured cars and submarines.

Eureka moment: Da Vinci showed that by drawing what he imagines, an inventor can inspire future generations to make these visions real.

SIR ISAAC NEWTON 1642 – 1727

Nationality: English

Profession: Mathematician

Biographical information: Newton went to Cambridge University in 1661, but his studies were interrupted by an outbreak of plague that closed the university for two years. During this period of enforced idleness, Newton did most of his best thinking. In 1667, he was appointed professor of mathematics at Cambridge.

- Most of his work is contained in his books *Principia Mathematica* (1687) and *Opticks* (1704).

Most famous discovery: Newton is best known for his theory of universal gravitation — that there is an attractive force between all the objects in the universe, and this force is called gravity. Newton used his theory to discover the mathematical laws that govern the motion of all the objects in the everyday universe. The movement of any object, be it a pick-up truck or a planet, can be explained and predicted by what is known as Newtonian physics.

- **See page 18 INVENTION OF THE TELESCOPE.**

Newton stories:

- Newton is supposed to have thought up the theory of gravitation after watching an apple fall from a tree.

- While studying light, Newton pushed blunt needles into the corners of his eyes to see what effect squashing his eyeballs had on his vision.

Other discoveries:

- A comprehensive theory of light that explained how lenses worked and how white light could be split into colours.

- A system of arithmetic called calculus.

- Newton built a reflecting telescope that used a curved mirror to give a better image.

Sir Isaac Newton

Franklin, Benjamin
American statesman, scientist and writer Benjamin Franklin was fascinated by the new discovery, electricity. In 1752, convinced that thunderstorms were electric, he proved it by flying a special kite into a storm. The lightning struck the kite and electricity travelled down the string. Franklin realised that buildings could be protected from thunderbolts if the electricity was conducted through a metal spike on the roof of a building to the ground via a thick wire. Franklin had invented a lightning conductor.

Galileo Galilei
Galileo was so intrigued by the swinging of the incense burner in Pisa's cathedral, he was inspired to work with pendulums. Galileo measured the time it took to make a complete swing and discovered that it took the same amount of time to get back to where it started, even when the size of the swing changed. Galileo experimented with pendulums for many years, but by the time he thought of using a pendulum's even swing to keep a clock running smoothly, he was old and totally blind.

Gillette, King C
Advised by a colleague to invent "something that would be used and thrown away", Gillette invented the disposable razor blade and new safety razor. Constantly having to buy new blades was not popular with customers, but never having to use a 'cut-throat' razor again was! Gillette founded his razor blade company in 1903.

Halley, Edmond
In 1717, English astronomer Edmond Halley invented the first diving bell in which people could stay under water for long periods. Earlier devices (primarily built for attempts to retrieve sunken treasure) had not been successful. Air was supplied to Halley's diving bell in barrels with weights to make them sink.

- **See page 18 HALLEY'S COMET.**

INVENTORS

A TO Z INVENTORS

Kwolek, Stephanie
Pound for pound, Stephanie Kwolek's invention Kevlar is five times stronger than steel. It is also chemical and flame resistant. Kevlar, best known for its use in bullet-resistant vests and crash helmets was developed in the 1960s when chemist Kwolek was working in the laboratory of US company DuPont Textiles.

Leclanché, Georges
In 1866, French engineer Leclanché invented the sealed, dry cell battery which is still used in many torches today. Until the invention of the Leclanché cell, people were restricted to Volta's battery which contained a liquid that had to be constantly topped up.

Mars, Frank
In 1911, Frank Mars and his wife Ethel began making and selling butter-cream sweets from their home in Tacoma, Washington, USA. In 1920, Frank invented the 'Mars bar' when he came up with the idea of producing malted chocolate milkshakes in a solid form that could be enjoyed anywhere.

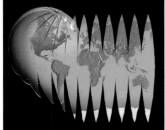

Mercator, Gerhard
In around 1568, Flemish cartographer Gerhard Mercator produced a map that gave sailors constant compass directions as straight lines. The 'Mercator projection' provided a flat, 'peeled' view of the globe. The map is very accurate for navigators, but showing the curved earth on flat paper causes distortions and makes countries at the Poles look too big.

JOHANNES GUTENBERG 1400 – 1468

Nationality: German

Profession: Jeweller/craftsman

Biographical information: Gutenberg was born in Mainz, and trained as a goldsmith. He lived and worked in Strasbourg between 1430 and 1444, then returned to Mainz.

Most famous invention: The process of printing with moveable type, and a printing press based on existing screw presses used to crush juice from grapes and olives.

Inventor at work: After 20 years of secret work to perfect all the necessary processes, Gutenberg printed and published his first book, a Latin Bible, in 1455. But money disputes with his financial backer, Johann Fust caused him to lose his business.

• See page 8 TIMELINE: PAPER AND PRINTING.

JOSEPH AND JACQUES MONTGOLFIER

Joseph: 1740 – 1810

Jacques: 1745 – 1799

Nationality: French

Profession: Paper-makers

Biographical information: The Montgolfier brothers worked in their father's paper factory in Annonay, France.

Most famous invention: The first hot air balloon. On 19 September, 1783, a sheep, a duck and a cockerel became the first living creatures to fly in free flight when they take off in a wicker basket suspended from a Montgolfier balloon.

On 21 November, 1783, Jean Francois Pilatre de Rosier and the Marquis d'Arlandes flew over Paris for 23 minutes in a Montgolfier balloon – the first human flight.

Eureka moment: Joseph and Jacques, noticed how flames sent scraps of paper floating up the chimney. They became convinced that a large bag filled with hot air would rise.

The Montgolfier balloon was made of fabric lined with paper. It was 10 m across.

• See page 29 TIMELINE: THE BALLOON INVENTORS.

SAMUEL MORSE 1791 – 1872

Nationality: American

Profession: Artist and inventor

Biographical information: Morse was born in Massachusetts. His father worked in the church and wrote geography books. Morse went to Yale College when he was 14 years old. He earned money painting pictures of his friends and teachers, and studied art in England becoming a well-known painter.

Most famous invention: Morse's interest in electricity led to his invention of the electrical telegraph and Morse code.

Eureka moment: Morse demonstrated his telegraph to the American Congress and, in 1843, they give him $30,000 to build a telegraph line from Washington D.C. to Baltimore

Other inventions: The bathometer which was used to find out how deep rivers and lakes were.

• See page 30 MORSE CODE.

LOUIS BRAILLE 1809 – 1852

Nationality: French

Profession: Teacher

Biographical information: Louis Braille was blinded at the age of three in an accident at his father's harness shop. In 1819, he went to the National Institute for Blind Children in Paris, and later became a teacher there. He died from tuberculosis.

Most famous invention: A system of reading and writing for the blind using raised dots in a six-dot matrix system. Braille's system was first published in 1829.

Eureka moment: At school in Paris, Braille learned of a system called *night writing* invented by Captain Charles Barbier for night-time battlefield communications.

In 1824, aged just 15, Braille developed his own system, using Barbier's as a starting point.

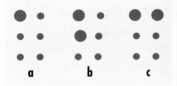

a   b   c

Braille is read using the fingertips.

THOMAS ALVA EDISON 1847 – 1931

Nationality: American

Profession: Inventor

Biographical information: After being expelled from school for stupidity, Edison was educated at home by his mother. He began experimenting with batteries and electricity when he was aged ten. He built his own telegraph and his first job was as a telegraph operator.

Most famous invention: Edison was already well known in the USA, but his 1877 invention of the phonograph made him world famous. The phonograph was the first device that could play pre-recorded music

Inventor at work: In 1876, Edison decided to become a full-time inventor. He built the world's first industrial research laboratory, which he called an *inventions factory*, at Menlo Park, New Jersey.

Other inventions: The most famous is the electric light bulb. Edison sometimes made as many as 400 inventions a year including the incandescent electric lamp, the microphone and the kinetoscope.

Edison patented 1,093 inventions during his life.

• *See pages 31 and 36 for more INFORMATION on Edison's inventing work.*

GEORGE EASTMAN 1854 – 1932

Nationality: American

Profession: Photographic film manufacturer

Biographical information: After leaving school, Eastman worked in insurance and banking while pursuing his hobby of photography. In 1880, he perfected a method of making photographic plates and set up a factory where he soon developed transparent film.

Most famous inventions: The first Kodak camera (Eastman invented the name Kodak and it became a trademark) which marked the beginning of amateur photography.

In 1900, Eastman launched the *Box Brownie* camera. It was so cheap, only one dollar including the film, that everybody could afford to buy one, making photography available to all.

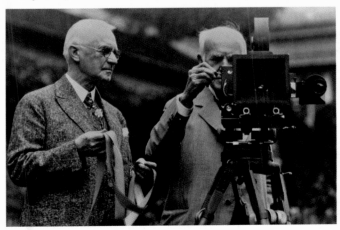

George Eastman (left) and Thomas Edison introduce colour motion pictures to the world in 1928.

• *See page 9 TIMELINE: INVENTION OF PHOTOGRAPHY*

• See pages 31 and 36 for more INFORMATION on Edison's inventing work.
• See page 9 TIMELINE: INVENTION OF PHOTOGRAPHY

A TO Z INVENTORS

Perignon, Dom
Benedictine monk Dom Perignon is credited with inventing champagne in around 1670, but other winemakers of the Champagne region of France probably contributed to its development. The special method of fermentation, known as 'méthode champenoise', produces the carbon dioxide which creates the bubbles loved by partygoers.

Richter, Charles F.
American seismologist Charles F. Richter developed his numbering system for measuring earthquakes in 1935. An earthquake measuring below 2 on the Richter scale would be recorded by equipment, but not felt by a person. An earthquake measuring 8 or more would be devastating.

Roosevelt, Theodore
While on a hunting expedition in 1902, US president Theodore 'Teddy' Roosevelt refused to shoot a defenceless bear cub. The story enhanced the popularity of the already popular president. Morris Michtom, a New York retailer cashed in on the incident by selling plush-covered bears with button eyes and jointed limbs. He called them 'Teddy's Bears'. A huge success, they soon became known as 'Teddy Bears'.

INVENTORS

Rubik, Erno
Hungarian design professor, Erno Rubik invented the Rubik's Cube. Popular during the early 1980s, over 150 million cubes were sold (100 million authorised units and 50 million imitations). Once twisted from its original arrangement, the puzzle had 43 quintillion possible configurations!

Schueller, Eugene
In 1936, French chemist Eugene Schueller produced the first suntan lotion at his company L'Oréal. Designer Coco Chanel made suntanning fashionable around this time. Today, the oil is sold around the world as Ambre Solaire.

Semple, William Finlay
On 28 December, 1869, William Semple of Mt Vernon, Ohio, USA, became the first person to patent a chewing gum – US patent 98,304.

Sinclair, Clive
In 1985, British inventor Clive Sinclair invented the C5, a battery-powered bike. The C5 had a top speed of 24 km/h, a range of 32 kilometres, and took eight hours to recharge the batteries. Unfortunately for Sinclair, consumers were not impressed with his new type of vehicle, and the invention flopped!

MARIE CURIE 1867 – 1934

Nationality: Polish

Profession: Physicist

Biographical information: Marie Sklodowska worked as a child-minder to support herself while she studied at university in Paris. In 1895, she married the French scientist Pierre Curie.

Most famous invention:
In 1898, the Curies discovered the radioactive elements radium, thorium and polonium named for Marie's homeland. In 1903, they shared the *Nobel Prize for Physics* with Henri

Becquerel. In 1911, Marie Curie was awarded the *Nobel Prize for Chemistry* for her continuing work on radium and radioactivity. Doctors found that radium could be used to treat cancer through radiotherapy.

Eureka moment: The discovery of radium involved breaking down and refining several tonnes of a mineral called pitchblende to locate less than one hundredth of a gram of pure radium.

Madame Curie poses in her Paris laboratory.

ALBERT EINSTEIN 1879 – 1955

Nationality: German-Swiss-American

Profession: Office clerk and mathematician

Biographical information: Einstein was born in Germany and attended college in Zurich, Switzerland. In 1901, he got a job at the Swiss Patent Office, and became a Swiss citizen. In his spare time he worked on difficult mathematical problems. When his work became well known, he returned to Germany. In 1933, he went to the USA and, in 1940, he became a US citizen.

Most famous discovery:
Somewhere among Einstein's maths is the simple formula $E=mc^2$. This means that matter (m) can be converted into energy (e), and that the amount of energy will be equal to the amount of matter times the speed of light (c) squared. The speed of light is about 300,000 km

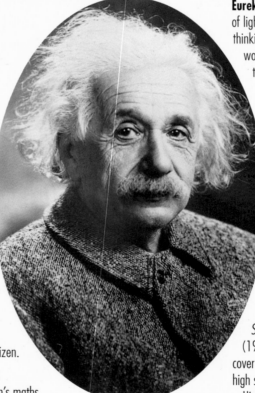

Albert Einstein

per second, so that mc^2 makes for an awful lot of energy. Einstein's formula summarises what happens when an atom bomb explodes.

Eureka moment: The speed of light was central to Einstein's thinking. One morning, travelling to work by bus, Einstein glanced at the Town Hall clock – if the bus suddenly accelerated to the speed of light, then the clock would appear to stop. The relative motion between observer and observed is at the heart of Einstein's two theories of relativity.

Other discoveries: Newton's laws of motion do not work mathematically for objects moving very quickly (near the speed of light). Einstein's *Special Theory of Relativity* (1905) extended the maths to cover objects moving at a constant high speed.

His *General Theory of Relativity* (1916) further extended the maths to cover rapidly accelerating objects. As well as showing that matter and energy were interconnected, Einstein also showed that space and time were interconnected, in a concept called *spacetime*.

ENRICO FERMI 1901 – 1954

Nationality: American
(born in Italy)

Profession: Physicist

Biographical information: Fermi studied physics at the University of Pisa and was awarded a doctorate for research into X-rays. He worked in Italy until he won the *Nobel Prize for Physics* in 1938. Fermi and his wife moved to Sweden and then to the USA.

Eureka moment: In 1939, Fermi realised that an atom bomb was possible. Together with other scientists, including Albert Einstein, he wrote to US President Franklin D. Roosevelt about the discovery. Roosevelt ordered the *Manhattan Project* (see page 10).

Most famous invention: Fermi designed and supervised the

1951 University of Chicago – Fermi at the controls of the new synchro-cyclotron built to study the origins of life.

construction of the world's first nuclear reactor. It was located in a basement squash court at the University of Chicago, USA.

Other inventions: Fermi discovered the first artificial element, neptunium (No. 93) and the element fermium (No.100) which is named in his honour.

• See page 10 NUCLEAR POWER for more information on the work of Enrico Fermi.

FRANCIS CRICK & JAMES WATSON

Crick: 1916—2004
Watson: born 1928

Nationality: English (Crick); American (Watson)

Profession: Molecular biologist (Crick); Biochemist (Watson)

Biographical information: Crick studied at Cambridge University, in England, and during World War II designed anti-shipping mines. Watson studied viruses at the University of Indiana, in the USA, where he received his doctorate in 1950.

Most famous discovery:
In 1953, while working at the Cavendish Laboratory in Cambridge, Crick and Watson discovered that the three-dimensional structure of the DNA molecule was a double helix.

• See page 15 THE STORY OF DNA

Crick (right) and Watson with their famous laboratory model of the DNA double helix.

Eureka moment: By 1950, scientists knew what DNA was made from, but they had no idea of its shape. Crick and Watson made many models of what they thought it might look like. Finally they came up with a double helix, shaped like a long, twisted ladder.

In 1962, they shared the *Nobel Prize for Medicine*.

A TO Z INVENTORS

Smith, Richard
Richard Smith, a blacksmith, carpenter and farmer encountered the problem of hard-to-remove tree stumps when turning forests into fields in South Australia. The stumps slowed the ploughing and broke ploughs. While ploughing one day in 1876, Smith observed that a plough-blade which had come loose rode over a stump and continued ploughing. Smith designed and manufactured the flexible 'Stump-jump' plough which had blades that were forced back into the soil by weights, after jumping.

Watson-Watt, Robert Alexander
In 1935, Scottish physicist Robert Alexander Watson-Watt was working on aircraft radio-location. He beamed radio waves at planes and then calculated the time it took to receive reflections back. Elapsed time gave him the aircraft's distance away. By late 1935, Watson-Watt was able to locate aircraft 110 kilometres away. His work led to the development of the first radar system.

Yale, Linus
In 1861, Linus Yale Jr. perfected the lock, with a compact revolving barrel and flat key, that we use today. It was based on a lock designed by his father using a principle known to the ancient Egyptians.

INVENTORS AT WORK

Some inventions are the result of years of dedicated research. Others come as a flash of inspiration. An invention may solve a specific problem, or be the by-product of an inventor's irresistible urge to understand how things work and then improve on them. All inventions draw on the accumulation of human knowledge and the work of earlier inventors. In this section of the book we take a brief look at a wide range of inventions. Many may not have made the headlines, but they represent the work of inventive men and women around the world.

ACUPUNCTURE

This ancient therapy is based on the idea that the life force or 'chi' flows in certain channels, which can become blocked. The practice of twirling a needle in the right place to make the 'chi' flow smoothly again has hardly changed since it was first used in China some 4,500 years ago. Thankfully, steel needles have now replaced stone ones!

ARCHIMEDES SCREW

A means of raising water for irrigation, the Archimedes screw comprises a cylinder with a large screw inside. The bottom of the screw is dipped in water and as the screw is turned, water is pushed up the cylinder. We don't know for sure if Archimedes actually invented this device or whether he saw it in use and wrote about it, but the device came to carry his name.

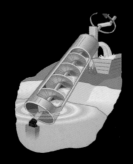

ARCHIMEDES SCREW

ADDER-LISTER

In 1888, US inventor William Burroughs patented an adding machine that printed its calculations. With more than 80 keys and a handle to operate the printer, the Adder-lister went on sale in 1892.

ADDING MACHINE

The arithmometer patented in 1820 by Frenchman Thomas de Colmar was the first calculating machine that really worked. It could add, subtract, multiply and divide. It took a while to catch on, and underwent many developments, but from the middle of the 19th Century, hundreds were in use.

AEROSOL CAN

Norwegian Erik Rothheim invented the aerosol can in the late 1920s for packaging paint and polish.

AIR CONDITIONING

In 1902, US engineer Willis Carrier designed an 'apparatus for treating air'. Carrier's invention was based on cooling the temperature until moisture condenses out, then draining away the water, to produce pleasantly cool, dry air.

AMALGAM FILLING

Before the early 1800s, metal tooth fillings were made by heating metal to boiling point before they were put into the tooth. Around 1826, working independently, August Taveau, in France, and Thomas Bell, in Britain, mixed mercury and silver to form a paste which they found could be inserted cold into the mouth and would harden quickly. The amalgam filling is still used today.

ASPIRIN

In 1899, German chemist Felix Hoffman re-discovered an old formula for a painkiller. The drug was aspirin which contains salicylic acid (juice from willow tree bark). Hoffman developed and tested the aspirin and used it to treat his father's arthritis. He patented Acetyl Salicylic Acid in 1900.

1899: ASPIRIN

BIKINI

In 1946, the bikini was invented independently by two Frenchmen Jacques Heim and Louis Reard. Heim designed a very small bathing suit he called the 'Atome' (french for atom), while Reard's creation was named the 'Bikini' after the place, the Bikini Atoll in the Marshall Islands, which was very much in the news at the time due to atom bomb testing taking place there.

BINGO

Originating in Europe, 'beano' as it was first called, arrived in the USA in 1929. Toy salesman, Edwin Lowe renamed the game 'bingo' after he heard someone accidentally call bingo instead of beano. Lowe hired a maths professor, Carl Leffler, to work out combinations for the bingo cards. Leffler eventually invented 6,000 different combinations. The game went on to be a popular means of fund-raising for the church.

BUBBLE GUM

In 1906, the first bubble gum, called 'Blibber Blubber' gum, was invented by Frank Fleer, but the chewy invention never went on sale. In 1928, Walter Diemer, an employee at Fleer's company invented the pink-coloured 'Double Bubble' bubble gum.

1946: BIKINI

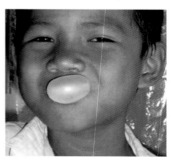

1906: BUBBLE GUM

BUBBLEWRAP

Bubblewrap appeared in 1960 in its earliest form as AirCap cellular cushioning. It consisted of two layers of soft plastic with bubbles trapped between them. Inventors Alfred Fielding and Marc Chavannes were originally trying to make textured wall covering!

CAMERA OBSCURA

The modern camera started as a darkened room with a tiny hole in one wall. It was called a camera obscura. On the opposite wall an upside down image of the outside world would appear. In 1558, Italian physicist Giovanni Battista Della Porta changed the hole for a lens which, by letting in more light produced a much sharper image. The Italian words 'camera obscura' mean 'a dark room'.

CAN-OPENER

Before 1855 a hammer and chisel were required to open cans. Then British inventor Robert Yeates

1855: CAN-OPENER

invented his can-opener – a sharp blade that was stuck in the top of a can, and then worked around.

CAT'S-EYES

The flexible rubber housing is the key to British engineer Percy Shaw's 1934 invention of 'cat's eyes'. It enables the reflectors, which light the centre of roads, to be cleaned by every car that crosses them.

CHAIN SAW

A petrol-engined sawing machine was made by German Emil Lerp in 1927. Although similar to a modern saw, it was too heavy for one person to lift. In 1950, the Stihl company produced the first chainsaw light enough for one person.

1927: CHAIN SAW

COMPTOMETER

Displaying its results in a set of windows, US engineer Dorr E. Felt's calculating machine was much faster than its rival the Burrough's Adder-lister which printed its results. Both machines were in use until the mid 20th century.

COTTON BUDS

This baby cleaning aid was introduced in the USA in 1926. Cotton buds were invented by Leo Gerstenzang after he saw his wife trying to use toothpicks and cotton wool.

DC06 ROBOT

Manufactured by Dyson, this robotic vacuum cleaner has sensors to help it avoid stairs and small children. It also remembers where it has cleaned!

DDT

The now little used insecticide DDT, a chlorine-based chemical, had been known for years before in 1939, a Swiss chemist Paul Muller discovered that it killed insects, but had little effect on warm-blooded animals.

DIVING SUIT

Augustus Siebe, a German engineer, invented the first practical diving suit in 1819. Siebe's suit comprised a jacket and an airtight helmet. Air was pumped into the helmet from the surface.

ELECTRON MICROSCOPE

Invented by Ernst Ruska in the 1930s, the electron microscope 'sees' with electrons rather than photons of light. Today's electron microscopes make it possible to view items as small as atoms and then display their image on a computer screen.

1930s: ELECTRON MICROSCOPE

ESCALATOR

The escalator can be credited to two inventors in the late 19th Century. Inventor George Wheeler sold his idea (because he had financial problems) to Charles Seeburger, a rival inventor. Seeburger then sold the patent to the Otis Company and the copyright to the name 'escalator' which he had created for the machine.

• See page 25
OTIS SAFETY LIFT.

FERRIS WHEEL

American George W. Ferris designed the first ferris wheel for the 1893 World's Fair in Chicago. Ferris was a bridge builder and owner of a company that tested iron and steel. The finished wheel had a diameter of over 75 metres. Thirty six wooden cars held up to 60 riders each. The price of a ride was 50 cents.

1893: FERRIS WHEEL

FIELD-ION MICROSCOPE

Invented by Erwin Mueller in 1956, the field-ion microscope has a magnification of more than 2.5 million times.

LAUGHING GAS

Although discovered earlier, in 1799 Humphry Davy found that nitrous oxide could make people laugh. He suggested it might be useful in surgery, but also used it to give party guests a good laugh!

LEMONADE

Lemon juice was probably used in drinks for many years before the first commercial lemonade was produced. In 1676, in Paris, vendors, belonging to the Compagnie de Limonadiers sold glasses of a mixture of lemon juice, honey and water. They dispensed the lemonade from tanks strapped to their backs.

LETTERBOX

On 4th October, 1892, American George Becket patented a letterbox for houses with a self-closing flap.

LIE DETECTOR

Originally developed by Czech psychologist Max Wertheimer in 1904, the polygraph, or lie detector, monitors blood pressure, pulse and breathing, all of which can change when people lie.

INVENTORS AT WORK

LIQUID PAPER

American secretary Bette Nesmith Graham invented liquid paper by mixing some of her artists' materials in her kitchen blender. When other secretaries noticed Bette using her invention to hide typing errors, they wanted some too! Bette started her 'Mistake out' company in 1956.

M&M's

M&M's were invented by snackfood genius Frank Mars (of Mars bar fame) in the 1930s. Frank wanted to invent a chocolate that had a protective candy coat to stop it melting.

1930s: M&Ms

MACADAMISED ROAD

In 1783, returning to his native Scotland after making his fortune in America, John McAdam took an interest in the poor state of the roads. He experimented with road surfaces and by 1815, using a mixture of different sized stones, he had perfected a waterproof, durable surface suitable for the coach traffic of the day.

MARGARINE

In 1869, the French chemist Hippolyte Mege-Mouries invented a butter-substitute called margarine by bubbling hydrogen through a mixture of vegetable oils.

MATCH

As knowledge of chemicals improved in the early 1800s, inventors used their knowledge to try to create an improved means of light (or match as we would call it today). In 1827, British chemist John Walker produced his 'Friction Lights' which lit up when rubbed on sandpaper.

MINER'S SAFETY LAMP

In the early 1800s, many lives were lost due to explosions in mines. The explosions were caused by the flames from miners' lights making the methane gas underground explode. Mine owners commissioned three men to try to find a solution: chemist Humphry Davy, William Clanny, a doctor, and mechanic George Stephenson. The mine owners were pleased with Davy's design, but the miners preferred the lamp designed by Stephenson, who was 'one of their own'. Eventually most miners' lamps incorporated ideas from all three inventors.

NEON SIGN

Inventors had discovered that low pressure gas in a tube could be lit up with electricity. In 1910, French physicist Georges Claude found that the gas neon produced an intense orange-red glow – not suitable for lighting, but great for advertising signs!

1910: NEON SIGN

NITROGLYCERINE

Discovered in 1846 by Italian chemist Ascanio Sobrero, nitroglycerine was the first 'high explosive' – an explosive much more powerful than gunpowder. Just dropping a container of the chemical on the floor can cause a large explosion.

OFRO ROBOT

Built by Robowatch Technologies, Germany, OFRO robots are designed to carry out surveillance in high security places, such as airports, nuclear power plants and prisons.

OIL PAINTING

Oil paint had been known about since Roman times, but until the early 15th century artists used paints such as tempera, which is made with eggs. The French and Flemish painters Robert Campin and Jan van Eyck perfected the use of oil paints in the 15th century. The graded tones that could be achieved with oil paints gave a greater sense of realism to their work.

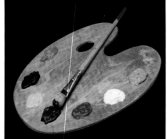

15th CENTURY: OIL PAINTING

OSCILLOSCOPE

A devise which makes it possible to see electrical signals on a screen. The cathode ray oscilloscope was invented in 1897 by German physicist Karl Ferdinand Braun.

PACKAGE HOLIDAY

The first 'package' holiday was in 1841 – a train trip from Leicester to Loughborough, in England. The excursion was a success. By 1855, the organiser, British missionary Thomas Cook, was organising trips to Europe.

PAPER CUP

In 1908, US inventor Hugh Moore designed a vending machine to deliver water in individual paper cups. Previously, thirsty consumers had to share a tin cup. Moore's paper cups became known as 'Dixies', named after the company set up to make them in 1919.

PARACHUTE

Frenchman Louis Lenormand gave his invention its first serious trial in December, 1783, by jumping from the Montpelier observatory with a 4.3 m chute. He landed safely. Although originally invented as a means of escaping a burning building, a parachute was used in 1797 by another Frenchman to jump to safety when his hot-air balloon burst over Paris!

PARKING METER

Businessman Carlton Magee's invention first appeared in Oklahoma City, USA, in 1935. Magee hoped his Park-O-Meter would stop all-day parkers taking up spaces on the streets, and make a little money for the city.

PENCIL

Having already identified graphite as a distinct mineral, in 1565 Conrad Gesner, a German-Swiss naturalist, had the idea of placing the carbon in a wooden holder to form a writing instrument. Modern pencils with a core of lead glued inside a thin tube of wood were first made in 1812.

1812: PENCIL

PEPSI-COLA

In 1893, Caleb Bradham a pharmacist in New Bern, North Carolina, USA, began experimenting with soft drink concoctions. Bradham's mixtures were sampled by customers at his drugstore. In 1898, one of his formulations known as 'Brad's Drink' proved popular and, on 28 August, it was re-named 'Pepsi-Cola'.

In 1902, the trademark was registered and the Pepsi-Cola Company was formed. In 1908, Pepsi was one of the first companies to start using motor vehicles instead of horse-drawn carts.

1893: PEPSI COLA

PLASTERS

In 1920, Earle Dickson, of US surgical dressing manufacturer Johnson and Johnson invented plasters. He stuck together adhesive tape, gauze and fabric and then rolled up the plasters for future use. Dickson's invention was soon on sale in the USA as Band-Aid.

PICK-PROOF LOCK

In 1784, British engineer Joseph Bramah offered £210 to anyone who could pick the lock he had invented. It was 67 years before the reward was claimed by US locksmith A.C. Hobbs, who took 51 hours to pick the lock.

POST-IT NOTE

US company 3M's Post-it notes were launched in 1980. A company chemist, Spencer Silver, made a 'not very sticky' adhesive, but it was his colleague Art Fry who suggested the use for it.

RAWLPLUG

Since 1919, when British builder John Rawlings devised his 'plug' there has been no need to damage walls when fixing into them. Rawlings invention means you simply drill a hole then insert a fibre rawlplug which expands to hold the screw.

RING-PULL CAN

The first drinks cans required a separate opener. In 1965, US engineer Ermal Fraze patented the convenient 'ring-pull' can. The sharp-edged ring-pulls could be dangerous if thrown away, so engineer Daniel Cudzik invented the 'stay-on tab'.

Robart III ROBOT

First made in 1992, Robart III is used by the US navy. It has a camera, infra-red sensor and also a gun that can fire darts. Robart III was built by Bart Everett of the Naval Oceans Systems Center.

RUBBER

French scientist Charles-Marie de la Condamine discovered rubber trees with their sticky sap while on an expedition to South America. Although other Europeans had come across the substance in their travels, it was la Condamine's samples, sent back to France in 1736, that put the product on the scientific map. Rubber was named when British chemist Joseph Priestley found that it would rub out pencil.

RUBBER BAND

In 1845, Stephen Perry of Messrs. Perry and Co. of London, England, a rubber manufacturing company, invented the rubber band. Perry used it to hold papers and envelopes together.

SAFETY PIN

US mechanic Walter Hunt invented the modern safety pin in 1849. His design was actually very similar to one that was invented and worn by people 2000 years ago. The clothing clasps were called fibulas, and they were used by the ancient Greeks and Romans for fastening clothing.

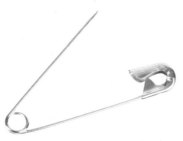

1849: SAFETY PIN

SCANNING TUNNELLING MICROSCOPE

Invented in Switzerland in 1981 by Gerd Binnig and Heinrich Rohrer, the scanning tunnelling microscope can be used to study and photograph individual atoms.

SCISSORS

The scissor principle was known in 3000 BC, but scissors like those we use today, with two blades pivoted at the centre, were invented by the Romans in about AD 100.

AD 100: SCISSORS

SHOPS

Ancient Greek historian Herodotus (c480 – 420 BC) stated, 'the people who invented coins also invented shops'. He may well have been referring to the Lydians (an ancient civilisation from the area that is now Turkey). The first shops were probably trading around 600 BC.

SLICED BREAD

Inventor Otto Frederick Rohwedder began work on a bread slicer in 1912. In 1928, he finally invented a machine that could slice bread and then wrap it to stop it going stale.

SLINKY

In 1943, engineer Richard James invented the 'Slinky' after he witnessed a long coil of metal (part of a Navy experiment) fall from a desk and appear to walk! He took the idea home to his wife Betty who named the toy Slinky after consulting her dictionary to find a word that described the spring's movement. To start off their new enterprise, Richard and Betty had just 400 springs made by a local machine shop. They soon needed to replenish their stock when the Slinky was a huge success!

SPECTACLES

The glass workers of Murano in Venice, Italy, invented the spectacles some time around AD 1275.

1275 AD: SPECTACLES

STEREOSCOPE

By combining two slightly different pictures, one for each eye, a three dimensional image is produced by a stereoscope. Invented before photography by Charles Wheatstone, stereoscopy became a craze after David Brewster showed a version of the stereoscope at the 'Great Exhibition', in London, in 1851.

STICKY TAPE

US engineer Richard Drew's first sticky invention was masking tape, a sticky paper tape. In 1925, by coating cellophane with a similar adhesive, he produced what is known in the USA by the trade name Scotch Tape, and in the UK as Sellotape.

SUPERGLUE

In 1951, US researchers Harry Coover and Fred Joyner realised the potential of the chemical cyanoacrylate (discovered in 1942) for use in a super-strong glue. A trace of water is all that is needed to trigger a chemical reaction which turns the liquid glue into plastic.

SUPERMARKET

In 1916, in order to cut costs in his business, US grocer Clarence Saunders invented 'self-service' at his Piggly Wiggly store in Memphis, Tennessee, USA. It was cheaper to let people take goods from the shelves than have staff members serve them. Saunders had invented the self-service supermarket!

1916: SUPERMARKET

SUPERMARKET TROLLEY

US retailer Sylvan Goldman noticed that customers at his Humpty Dumpty supermarkets never purchased more than they could carry. In 1937, he had wheels and baskets welded to folding chairs and the supermarket trolley was born.

SURGICAL GLOVES

Convinced that germs were a threat to their patients, 19th century surgeons needed to find a way to keep their hands sterile while operating. In 1890, US surgeon William Halsted invented thin rubber surgeons' gloves and the problem was solved.

THERMOS FLASK

Based on James Dewar's vacuum bottle, Rheinhold Burger's metal-cased flask was launched in 1904. The name Thermos flask was chosen after a competition.

TOOTHPASTE IN A TUBE

'Crème Dentifrice', produced in 1892 by US dentist Washington Sheffield, was the first toothpaste to come in a tube. Before Sheffield's innovation, toothpaste had come in a jar.

TRAFFIC SIGNAL

An early form of traffic lights appeared in London in 1868. In 1923, a system using three moving arms was patented in the USA by inventor Garrett Morgan.

TRAMPOLINE

Circus acrobat and Olympic medallist, George Nissen invented the trampoline in 1936. He built a prototype in his garage and later patented the idea.

TRIVIAL PURSUIT

Described as 'a party in a box' and a 'revolt against television', the quiz game Trivial Pursuit was devised by four Canadian friends in 1979. After a slow start, the marketing took off when the game was launched in the USA. In 1984 alone, more than 20 million games were sold!

TYPEWRITER

American mechanical engineer, Christopher Sholes patented the first practical typewriter in 1868. Sholes laid the keyboard out in the pattern which is known as QWERTY – after the six letters that appear top left on the keyboard. This layout was designed to slow down the typist, in order to stop the keys jamming. Modern keyboards still have the same layout.

UMBRELLA

The steel-ribbed umbrella that we know today was invented in England in 1874 by Samuel Fox.

1874: UMBRELLA

VACUUM CLEANER

In 1901, British engineer and inventor, Hubert Cecil Booth invented the vacuum cleaner. Booth's large, horse-drawn machine went from house to house sucking out the dirt through hoses. Booth formed the British Vacuum Cleaner Company in 1903, and built his first canister-style machine in 1904.

1979: TRIVIAL PURSUIT

VELCRO

Patented in the 1950s, Swiss inventor George de Mestral's invention of Velcro came to him after tiny plant burrs (seed pods) attached themselves to his clothes and his dog while hiking in the countryside. Under the microscope the burrs were discovered to have tiny hooks which were hooked in the fabric of Mestral's trousers. Mestral's idea was to produce a two-sided fastener with hooks on one side and soft loops on the other – Velcro. The name Velcro is a combination of two French words, velours (velvet) and crochet (hook).

VELOCIPEDE

The 'draisienne' invented by Baron Karl von Drais de Sauerbrun in 1817, is recognised as the first two-wheeled, rider-propelled machine. Although von Drais called his device a Laufmaschine (running machine), draisienne and velocipede became more popular names. Made of wood, the machine was propelled by the seated rider paddling his feet on the ground. Copies were soon being made in other countries and, in 1818, Denis Johnson of London patented a 'pedestrian curricle' which was an improved version of the draisienne.

VENDING MACHINE

Drop in a coin and the machine will release a shot of holy water. Ancient Greek inventor, Hero of Alexandria described this early type of vending machine in a book around AD 60. It is not known if the machine was ever built.

WINDSURFER

Norman Darby's passion for boatbuilding led to his invention of the sailboard or windsurfer. One day in 1943 while out sailing, Norman wanted to cross a stretch of very shallow water. First he removed the keel of his small boat and then the rudder. He found that he could steer by tilting the sail. From that moment he worked to perfect a purpose-built board.

ZODIAC SIGNS

The Mesopotamians were very keen star-gazers. Around 500 BC, Astronomer-priests divided the night sky into 12 equal parts and identified each part by a different star constellation. The constellations they recognised are the basis of modern-day star signs and horoscopes.

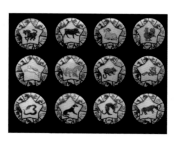

500 BC: ZODIAC SIGNS

WHAT IS A PATENT?

To prevent other people from making, using, or selling an invention without the inventor's permission, he or she must apply to a government patent office to take out a patent.

- If no one else has patented the same invention, a patent will be granted for a specific period of time. Patents usually cover the way things work, what they do, how they are made, and what they are made of.

- Today, most patents are granted to cover newly invented improvements to existing technology.

INVENTORS AT WORK

FAMOUS PATENTS

- US Patent No. 1,647
  20 June, 1840
  Samuel Morse
  Telegraph
- US Patent No. 13,661
  9 October, 1855
  Isaac Singer
  Sewing machine
- US Patent No. 223,898
  27 January, 1880
  Thomas Edison
  Electric light
- US Patent No. 686,046
  5 November, 1901
  Henry Ford
  Automobile

- US Patent No. 821,393
  22 May, 1906
  O. & W. Wright
  Airplane
- US Patent No. 1,773,079
  12 August, 1930
  Clarence Birdseye
  Packaged frozen food

IT SEEMED LIKE A GOOD IDEA AT THE TIME...

BLAST OFF!
In 1500, Chinese scientist Wan Hu tried to fly by tying 47 rockets to his sedan chair. The rockets exploded, and he was never seen again!

Sometimes inventors are convinced that they HAVE actually found the best thing since Otto Rohwedder's sliced bread – it's just that nobody else appreciates their genius!

Here are a selection of inventions which, for some reason, did not make it into production...

AIR-COOLED ROCKING CHAIR
On 6 July, 1869, US Patent No. 92,379 was issued to Charles Singer for his innovative, breezy rocking chair. The chair was to have bellows (devices that were once used for blowing air onto fires) connected to a hose that blew air onto the sitter as he or she rocked.

THE VÉLO-DOUCHE
In 1897, an English bicycle manufacturer contemplated the idea of a 'Vélo-douche shower bath' – an exercise bike combined with a shower to keep the rider clean and fit.

A CUTE INVENTION
On 19 May, 1896, US Patent No. 560,351 was issued to inventor Martin Goetze for his device for producing and maintaining dimples on human skin.

SNOW TO AUSTRALIA
About 35 years ago, an intriguing idea was patented in the UK by inventor A.P. Pedrick. The idea was to irrigate the Australian desert by using the force from the spin of the Earth to pipe snow and ice balls from Antarctica.

CHEWING GUM LOCKET
On 1 January, 1889, US Patent No. 395,515 was issued to Christopher W. Robertson for his invaluable invention, the chewing gum locket. Conveniently stashed away in the locket, chewed gum could be safely carried on the person. Far better than leaving it around to get dirty or, more importantly, *"found and chewed by someone with an ulcerous or diseased mouth"*!

PATENT PROBLEMS

In theory it should be very simple to patent your idea. However, in practice, it can sometimes be a long and expensive process if people try to steal your idea, or claim they had it before you.

- Alexander Graham Bell filed his patent application for the telephone on 7 March, 1876, only hours before his rival Elisha Gray.

- Gray pursued Bell with 600 lawsuits claiming the idea.

CONCRETE FURNITURE

In 1911, American inventor Thomas Edison proposed a new range of home furnishings made from concrete.

- Easy to manufacture and low in cost, Edison's special lightweight concrete would be used to produce phonograph cabinets, pianos and even bedroom furniture.

- Unfortunately, when Edison shipped some phonograph cabinets to a trade show they arrived in pieces — not good publicity for a product marketed as being able to withstand being dropped and abused!

- The world was not ready for Edison's new idea, and concrete furniture faded into history.

WORDS OF WISDOM

"Results...
...I have gotten a lot of results. I know several thousand things that won't work."

Thomas Alva Edison
Inventor

GLOSSARY

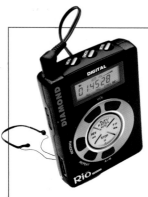

AIDS (Autoimmune Deficiency Syndrome) A fatal disease caused by HIV that renders victims susceptible to infections and cancers. AIDs can be slowed, but not cured, by expensive drugs.

Alternating current The flow of electricity supplied to homes and offices through electrical mains. It reverses direction about 50 or 60 times per second.

Anatomist Medical scientist who studies the bones, organs and other structures that make up an animal body.

Anthropologist Someone who studies the traditional human societies and cultures that still exist in the modern world.

Archaeologist Someone who seeks out and studies non-written evidence of past human cultures and civilisations.

Atom Smallest possible unit of a chemically pure element. All materials and substances are composed of atoms and combinations of atoms known as molecules.

Atom bomb Device that uses the chain reaction of uranium or plutonium to produce an extremely powerful explosion. A single atom bomb is equivalent to a million tonnes of ordinary explosive.

Atomic size The atomic size of an element depends on the number of protons and neutrons in the nucleus. An atom of hydrogen has just one proton in the nucleus; an atom of uranium has 92

protons and even more neutrons.

Australopithecus (Southern ape) One of a group of bipedal (using two legs) primates that lived in Africa about 4 million years ago, and which may have been the ancestors of modern human beings.

Base pairs The four nucleotide bases – thymine (T), guanine (G), cytosine (C), and adenine (A) – that make up the genetic code. They are always arranged in pairs.

Biochemist Scientist who studies the substances produced by living things and how they combine and react with other substances.

BASIC (Beginners All-purpose Symbolic Instruction Code) A computer language that is used to write operating programmes for a computer.

Bacteria Group of single-celled organisms that are similar to the earliest forms of life. Bacteria do not have a nucleus and do not use DNA. Some bacteria cause diseases.

Binary Using just two digits, 1 and 0. Computers operate according to instructions written in binary numbers. Text and other information (such as sound and video) can be digitised (converted into binary numbers) for storage or transmission.

Botanist A scientist who studies plants.

Calculus A type of arithmetic used to find the solution to problems where there are two variable quantities, as in the complex motion of a cannonball through the air, or a planet through space.

Cathode ray tube A hollow glass device that 'fires' a stream of electrons from one end so that they form an image on the flattened surface of the other end. The cathode ray tube is the basis for ordinary TV sets.

Census A count of the total population of a country. Many governments conduct a census every ten years.

Centrifugal force The force that appears to make objects on a rotating body move toward the outer edge.

Clone A plant or animal produced from a single cell that is an absolutely identical copy of the plant or animal from which the cell was taken. A clone has exactly the same DNA as the 'parent'.

Co-axial cable Electrical communications cable with an insulated central strand of thick metal wire surrounded by a woven mesh of fine wires.

Current The 'flow' of electricity around a circuit.

Cyclotron A device used to accelerate sub-atomic particles (such as protons, neutrons, or electrons) so that they crash into each other to produce other sub-atomic particles.

Dialysis medical technique for removing harmful chemicals from the blood of patients with kidney failure.

Digital Stored or transmitted in digital form – as a series of binary numbers.

Direct current (DC) Electricity, produced by batteries and dynamos, that flows unidirectionally from a positive anode to a negative cathode.

DNA (Deoxyribonucleic acid) The substance which contains the genetic code used to pass on characteristics to offspring. All living things except bacteria use DNA, and every species has its own type of DNA molecule.

Electro-magnet A device that only exhibits magnetism when an electrical current is applied to it.

Electron Sub-atomic particle with a negative electrical charge. Electrons orbit around the nucleus of atoms. An atom usually has the same number of electrons as protons in its nucleus.

Electron shell The orbit of electrons around an atomic nucleus forms a series of hollow, spherical 'shells', one inside the other with the nucleus at the centre.

Element One of the pure chemical substances. There are 92 naturally occurring elements, and about 20 short-lived artificial elements that have been made in laboratories.

ESA (European Space Agency) A multinational organisation concerned with space exploration and research.

Exposure time Length of time a camera shutter remains open in order to produce an image of the desired quality.

Fibre-optic cable Communications cable, made from woven strands of glass, designed to carry messages as pulses of laser light.

Font A set of the letters of the alphabet and the numerals in matching size and style. Printers use a great many fonts when producing books and magazines – two fonts have been used in this glossary.

Genes The means by which characteristics are inherited through DNA. A gene is a section of the genetic code that contains the instructions for one specific thing, such as making a particular protein.

Genome The complete genetic code for a particular species.

HIV (Human Immunodeficiency Virus) The microscopically small substance that causes AIDs (Autoimmune Deficiency Syndrome). HIV is spread from person to person through sexual contact and the use of illegal drugs.

Homo erectus Early type of human that lived between 1 and 2 million years ago. Some scientists believe that Homo erectus was a direct ancestor of modern humans.

Internet An international network of computers developed in the 1970s. The Internet is now used commercially and can be accessed by all computer users.

Jurassic Period in earth's history from 208 to 146 million years ago. During the Jurassic period dinosaurs lived on land.

Meteorologist A scientist who studies the weather.

Microchip A component of electronic devices, also known as an integrated circuit or silicon chip. A microchip is a small wafer of silicon with thousands of tiny electrical circuits on its surface.

Microprocessor A component of electronic devices. A microprocessor is a self-contained microchip that can perform several electronic tasks at the same time.

Minoans Ancient inhabitants of the island of Crete who developed the first civilisation in Europe around 2,500 BC. The Minoan capital was the great palace at Knossos.

Morse Code Sequence of dots and dashes representing letters and numbers invented by Samuel Morse and used to transmit messages by flashes of sunlight on a mirror (heliograph) or along electrical wires (telegraph).

NASA (National Aeronautics and Space Administration) The US government agency responsible for space exploration and research.

Negative In photography a negative is an intermediate stage produced from exposed film. In a negative image the colours and tones of the original scene are reversed so that light is dark and dark is light. A bright light is then shone through the negative onto light-sensitive paper to produce a positive image.

Neolithic (New Stone Age) Period of human prehistory when people developed farming and pottery. In Europe and Asia the Neolithic period lasted from 12,000 to 7000 years ago.

Neutron A sub-atomic particle. A component of atomic nuclei that has no electrical charge.

Nuclear reactor A device that uses radioactive material (such as uranium or plutonium) to produce a slow, heat-generating chain reaction. Nuclear reactors are used in atomic power stations.

Nucleotide bases Four chemical substances – thymine (T), guanine (G), cytosine (C), and adenine (A) – that are linked together one after the other to form the long strands of the DNA molecule. The genetic code is often said to be a code written in just four letters T, G, C, and A.

Nucleus The central part of an atom or cell. In atoms the nucleus is formed of protons and neutrons. In a cell, the nucleus normally contains DNA.

Oscilloscope Device that uses a cathode-ray tube to show electrical signals as glowing lines on a glass screen. Oscilloscopes are used to monitor frequency, wavelength, signal strength etc.

Ozone Form of the gas oxygen normally found in the upper levels of Earth's atmosphere where it forms a barrier against ultraviolet radiation.

PALEOLITHIC (Early Stone Age) Period of human prehistory when people made cutting implements and other tools from stone. The Paleolithic period lasted from around 2.5 million to 20,000 years ago.

Paleontologist Someone who studies the fossilised remains of prehistoric animals.

Phoenicians People who lived along the eastern coast of the Mediterranean about 3,000 years ago. They were traders and seafarers and, in around 800 BC, they founded the city of Carthage in present-day Tunisia.

Photograph Image of reality captured by a light-sensitive medium (for example, photographic film), which can be printed onto a sheet of paper.

Photographic plate Sheet of metal or glass coated with light-sensitive chemicals that was used in cameras before the invention of transparent plastic film.

Physicist Scientist who studies the physical properties of substances, and the way that objects of all sizes are affected by force and energy.

Physiologist Medical scientist who studies the operation and activity of the organs in a healthy body.

Plate tectonics The natural mechanism by which the large plates of solid rock that make up the earth's outer crust 'float' on the semi-solid rock beneath and gradually change their position.

Positive In photography a positive image is one in which colour tones have the same values as the original scene.

Primeval atom Phrase invented to name the unknown and incredibly small state of the universe immediately preceding the *Big Bang* that created the Universe, as we know it, around 15 billion years ago.

Protein Type of substance produced by living things. Proteins are used to build the structures of cells and tissue.

Proton Sub-atomic particle. A component of atomic nuclei that has a positive electrical charge.

Prototype Trial version of a device intended for manufacture.

Protozoa Single-celled animals living in soil and water that are much more highly developed than bacteria.

Radioactivity Harmful emissions from certain substances, such as radium, uranium, and plutonium that are said to be radioactive. There are three types of radioactivity: alpha rays, beta rays, and gamma rays that are composed of sub-atomic particles such as neutrons, protons, and high-energy photons.

Radiometric dating Method of establishing the age of rocks by measuring the rate at which radioactive substances lose their radioactivity.

Resistance The degree to which a material allows electricity to flow through it without losing energy in the form of heat.

Restriction enzyme Substance used to cut the long-stranded DNA molecule into short strands that each contains just a few genes.

Semiconductor Substance such as silicon that conducts electricity in a variable and controllable manner. Semiconductors are widely used to make transistors and microchips.

Shadowgraph Outline or silhouette image produced by blocking light from reaching a photo-reactive surface.

Solar-powered Driven by electricity produced from sunlight.

Speed of light Approximately 300,000 kilometres per second. Light travels at slightly different speeds through different media, for example a vacuum, air or water. The speed of light through a vacuum is a constant throughout the universe.

Stereoscopic Providing images that have depth (like those provided by a pair of eyes) as opposed to the flat images produced by cameras with a single lens.

Transistor A transistor is a component of an electronic circuit that depends upon the variable conductivity of a semiconductor. Transistors are very small compared with the triode valves and vacuum tubes that they replaced.

Triode valve Fragile glass and metal device used in radios and other electronic devices before the invention of the transistor.

Ultrasound imaging Medical technique for providing images of the inside of a living body by using reflected sound waves.

Vacuum tube A component of early electronic circuits. A vacuum tube was a hollow glass device containing complex arrangements of bare wires. The air inside the tube was evacuated leaving a vacuum so that the wires did not burn out when they became hot during use.

White light Sunlight, which can be split into the colours of the rainbow by refraction through a glass prism and through raindrops.

INDEX